IDAHO
100

C.C. Anderson tossing coins for children in Boise. (Photo courtesy, Boise First United Methodist Church, The Cathedral of the Rockies)

IDAHO 100

The people who most influenced the Gem State

Randy Stapilus
Martin Peterson

Ridenbaugh Press
2012

Copyright © 2012 Randy Stapilus and Martin Peterson

All Rights Reserved.

No part of this book may be reproduced, stored in a retrieval system, or transmitted in any form by any means, without prior permission of the publisher.

Composition and editing by Ridenbaugh Press, Carlton, Oregon.

Cover design by Randy Stapilus.

Library of Congress Cataloging-in-Publication Data:

Stapilus, Randy

Peterson, Martin

    Idaho 100: The People Who Most Influenced the Gem State

    Includes bibliographical references

    ISBN 978-0-945648-01-7(softbound)

    1. Idaho. 2. Politics 3. Geography 4. Business. I. Title.

Printed in the United States of America.

October 2012

10 9 8 7 6 5 4 3 2 1

Contents

	Introduction	1
1	Lloyd Adams	6
2	Elias Davidson Pierce	12
3	Ira Perrine	15
4	William Clagett	17
5	Joe Marshall	19
6	James Ailshie	21
7	Tom Roach	23
8	Thomas Ricks	25
9	Fred T. Dubois	27
10	Wetxuwiis	30
11	John R. Simplot	32
12	William Deary	34
13	William Budge	36
14	Frank Church	38
15	Frank Fenn	41
16	Cecil Andrus	43
17	Edward Stevenson	46
18	Robert Smylie	49
19	Joe Albertson	52
20	Bill Johnston	54
21	Frank Gooding	56
22	Ray Smelek	58
23	James McClure	60
24	C.W. Moore	62
25	Lafayette Cartee	64
26	C.A. Robins	66
27	Ezra Taft Benson	68
28	George Grimes/Moses Splawn	70
29	Harry Day	73
30	Duane Hagadone	75
31	Moses Alexander	77
32	Francois Payette	79

33	Lawyer	81
34	Pinckney Lugenbeel	83
35	Charles Rich	85
36	Gwen Barnett	87
37	William Craig	89
38	J.M. Guffey	91
39	Eugene Chaffee	93
40	James Hawley	95
41	William Dewey	97
42	Tom Boise	99
43	Harry Morrison	102
44	Drew Standrod	104
45	Frank F. Johnson	106
46	David Thompson	108
47	C. Ben Ross	111
48	Don Chance/Cal Williams	113
49	Frank Steunenberg	116
50	Calvin Cobb	118
51	William Judson Boone	128
52	William D. Haywood	130
53	Permeal French	133
54	John Haines	136
55	Willis Sweet	138
56	Lynn Driscoll	140
57	Harry Magnuson	142
58	Georgia Davidson	144
59	Michael Jordan	147
60	Clifford Strike	149
61	Erwin Graue	151
62	Bill Campbell	153
63	David Ballard	155
64	John Hailey	157
65	Verda Barnes	159
66	Ernie Day/Bruce Bowler	162
67	James "Doc" Taylor	164
68	Myran Schlechte	167
69	William Borah	169
70	C.C. Van Arsdol	171
71	Hummel/Tourtellotte	173
72	Perry Swisher	175

73	Alfred Budge	178
74	Phil Reberger	180
75	Andrew Little	182
76	John Evans	184
77	Charles McDevitt	186
78	Aaron Parker	189
79	Thomas Humbird	191
80	George Yost	193
81	Ron Twilegar	195
82	John B. Neil	197
83	Bill Roden	199
84	H. Westerman Whillock	201
85	AD Foote/AJ Wiley	203
86	Dick Eardley	205
87	Boyd Martin	207
88	Richard Butler	209
89	George Shoup	211
90	Phil Batt	213
91	Ernie Stensgar	215
92	Alonzo Leland	217
93	William J. McConnell	219
94	Nathan Falk	221
95	Len B. Jordan	223
96	Hill Beachy	225
97	Richard Z. Johnson	227
98	Carl E. Brown	229
99	C.C. Anderson	231
100	Merle Wells	233

50 honorable mentions	235
Timeline	252
Bibliography	256

Photo pages   *120*

Introduction

We all make our contributions, of one sort or another, to the place we live. They may be small. They may be large.

One of the authors' neighbor families lives at the entrance to a city park, and in recent years they have planted a small self-made sculpture garden in their yard. It isn't a big deal. But it has an effect: People who enter the park, as thousands do over the year, see the sculpture garden, and their sense of the park and the city are subtly altered by what they see. It may affect their sense of what they might do in the park, or how to appreciate it. It might have a sliver of an effect on city residents whose taxes fund the park's upkeep, and on city officials who specifically decide what happens there.

We all leave tracks behind, many of them readily visible only to family, friends, and associates, some of them (often anonymously) apparent to people unknown. Most of these things we do result in change on the small scale.

This book is about certain things that people did – in Idaho – that resulted in large-scale change; in the way people live and work in Idaho over an extended period of time. It lists 100 of the foremost actors who helped make Idaho what it is; we hope it will offer an accessible insight into just how this state developed.

We draw here this attention to actions, rather than to people, to underline a critical point.

This book isn't about the 100 greatest Idahoans, or the best Idahoans, or the most famous.

It isn't an honor roll.

It's an encapsulation of what people did that has transformed Idaho, for good and for bad. And opinions will differ, in some cases, on which is which. Amount of impact is at least a little more definable, and a little less grist for value judgments, than assessments of positive and negative.

The people who had the largest impact on Idaho in effect shaped large pieces of its history. And when looked at this way, Idaho's history takes on a different character from the way many histories present it.

Hindsight can make anything look inevitable, but little about the history of Idaho (or anywhere else) is inevitable. True, there are broad-brush aspects to Idaho history that almost certainly would have happened regardless what any one individual did. There's almost no way Idaho would have remained without cities and towns in the new millennium, for example. Even if none of the 100-plus people in this book had ever lived, Idaho, or perhaps an entity in the same location but under a different name, would exist.

But many of the details, large and small, might have been different. What are now the Pacific Northwest states could have wound up as British, and then Canadian. The Idaho Panhandle might have been developed much earlier, or later. Potatoes were not an inevitably Idaho-associated crop. Boise might not have been founded anywhere near where it was (in which event it could have been named something else), and it might have developed on very different lines. Many of the people who live in eastern Idaho today are members of the Church of Jesus Christ of Latter-day Saints (Mormons); that portion might, with a few slight historical twists, have been far smaller. The Magic Valley, known to early travelers as a bitter desert region, could have remained so. That each of these developments and more happened as they did, can be attributed in considerable part to the actions of a relatively small number of specific people.

They call this kind of speculation counterfactual history, a consideration of what might have happened if one minor turning point, at a critical juncture, had gone the other way. (It's a popular sub-genre in fiction.) This book doesn't emphasize the counterfactual side – our interest is in history as it actually happened – but we employed the exercise from time to time. What would have happened had this person not been there? Would someone else almost certainly have done the same thing, or might the result have been very different?

A person had to be in some way transformational – changing, even if in subtle ways, the world around – to qualify for inclusion on the list of the 100.

We considered whether what a person did would have almost certainly happened, in a similar way, in any case. Sometimes, however, the fact that something happened in a specific time and place was itself important, and that was factored in, too.

Another concept we considered was *reverberation* – what were the after effects of what the person did? Did the person's actions lead to other actions, and others beyond, or did their impact stop with themselves? Consider the Case of Elias Pierce, ranked high on this list. His main Idaho-related achievement was launching the first Idaho gold rush. That by itself was important, but more significantly, it brought people into what is now Idaho, in the Clearwater River valley, and the ripple effects sent them south, to the Florence area, to the Boise Basin, to the Owyhees, to the Wood River Valley. Pierce's specific achievement was limited; the after-effects were enormous.

We also tried – but didn't always limit ourselves – to stick to what was readily traceable, leaving aside as far as we could speculation.

These are some of the standards we considered when placing people on this list. Here are some others.

The list is limited to people whose names are available. If we know that at some time in the past an important action was undertaken by one person, that person isn't here unless we know the name, and have at least good reason to believe he or she existed.

We limited the list to Idahoans, and to people whose actions had specific local effect on Idaho. By "Idahoan" we mean someone who lived in the state, long enough to – in modern terms – declare residency, possibly to vote, at least long enough to obtain a drivers license (though of course many of these people lived before there were such things). People who simply traveled through Idaho (probably most famously, Lewis and Clark), or vacationed but did not establish a residence, don't qualify. And by "local effect" we mean an impact that hits Idaho in a specifically statewide, local or regional way. Philo Farnsworth, the principal inventor of television, grew up in Rigby and even conceived some of the principles he would use in designing video tubes while there. But most of his work along those lines was done elsewhere, and the impact of television is international, in no way limited to the Idaho area. (We note him, however, in a section after the main list.)

We eliminated from consideration people currently in public office, and generally (there are two or three limited exceptions) people still active in their careers at the time of writing. Not only are their eventual contributions too hard to properly evaluate, but there's no chance to see their aftermath – what followed their actions.

There's no attempt here to shape the list demographically or otherwise. The overwhelming majority of the people on it are, simply, white men; there are few women, and few from ethnic minorities. Here we get into the differences between kinds of change, and change on the individual and social level. Have women, Native Americans and other segments of society played a big role in shaping Idaho? Of course they have. But relatively few as individuals had the kind of sweeping impact that add them to the list here. For much of Idaho history public offices were filled almost exclusively by white men, and white men ran the businesses and led the pioneer parties. Until relatively recently, they've had a near-monopoly on those kinds of jobs. That's history.

There's no specific attempt at geographic balance, either, though geography plays different roles for different people.

Some people's actions exerted influence over the whole state, or much of it, and others had impact in a region, or even just a county or city. We included people here based on a calculus of influence: Relatively modest impact that was statewide might equal a larger impact on a community, for example. (Carl Brown's influence was essentially limited to the city of McCall, but there it was simply vast.) The principle applies to time as well: The impact of some people has run for a long time, in a few cases since before territorial days, and for others it was relatively brief, either starting and stopping years ago, or starting in the relatively recent past. Time span of impact is taken into account too.

What about cases where the actions involved really concerned two or three people, making it difficult to single out just one individual? We do have a few joint entries (meaning that the number of individual people on the list actually is more than 100). The rules for the people in joint entries are the same as for the others, except that what they did had to be something they worked on together, where the contribution of one cannot be separated from the contribution of the other. They had to be more than just two people working in the same field at the same time; they had to be, in some respect, collaborators.

The 100 are listed in rank order – from "most influential" on down.

After the list of 100, we've thrown in another list of 50, people who had some real and major effect on the state, some close calls for the 100, others important but disqualified in some way.

Some of them might have qualified for the 100 except that we ran out of numbers first – those in the 100 were simply more influential. Some didn't qualify for the 100 because of residency or other considerations, but we felt that what they did merit mention. (Hello, Philo.)

Our list may not be the same as yours – and probably won't be. That's good. If we kick up a few arguments about how Idaho got this way, and maybe even about what it might be, our job is well accomplished.

Randy Stapilus
Martin Peterson
September 2012

Acknowledgements

We should note that one of the inspirations for this book is *The 100: A Ranking of the Most Influential Persons in History*, by Michael H. Hart. Its criteria are roughly similar to most of ours, but applied worldwide. First published in 1978, it was redone (with some changes in the rankings) in 1992. His "most influential" in human history is Muhammad, second is Isaac Newton, and third is Jesus Christ. We won't go into Hart's rationale here, but just suggest that if you're intrigued at all, read the book. It's available on Amazon.com (and probably elsewhere).

We should like thank the people who provided help and counsel for us as we worked on the book, and read through the near-final version before we went to press. Judy Austin (who helped greatly throughout and especially on the Foote/Wiley entry), Jim Weatherby, Marty Trillhaase, John Hecht, Mark Mendiola all helped tremendously.

Insights into individuals and events were greatly assisted by conversations and correspondence with a wide range of individuals, including the late Perry Swisher, Sal Celeski, Michael Southcombe, Charles McDevitt, Myran Schlechte, Susan Stacy, Neal Parsell, Bob Krueger, and Kristin Ford, among many others.

In addition, a great deal of thanks to the staffs of the Idaho State Archives, the Boise Public Library, the University of Idaho Library's Special Collections and the Idaho Legislative Library for their assistance in this effort. More and more people today, we included, are getting information from the Internet. But the Internet will never replace the availability of hard copy and other resources – and the people – in our libraries.

1 W. Lloyd ADAMS

April 25, 1885-August 14, 1969. Attorney, lobbyist, journalist. State senator. Rexburg. Rexburg cemetery.

Lloyd Adams was the pre-eminent fixer in Idaho for half a century, and its pre-eminent political builder as well.

Journalist and politician Perry Swisher (who also appears on this list) remarked in a 1966 column, "The magic of Lloyd Adams' stratagems may be traced through Idaho history back to World War One, and it continues. Adams is a card file of 50 years of situations, tactics, victories and mistakes, personalities and platforms, headlines and whispers. The man is complex; experience taught Adams to disguise the speed and diversity of his intellect from politicians who, in the main, shy away from too much brilliance ... He has helped to make and guide many Idaho governors, senators, congressmen, and appointive administrators. John Thomas, Frank Gooding, William E. Borah, D. Worth Clark, Charles Gossett, all made great use of him as governors and senators. To bring the list up to date would be indelicate."

Adams was – by design – the invisible man, or nearly so; his name will be unfamiliar to most Idahoans, and he hardly shows up in Idaho history books. This was part of his design. When in 1935 the state of Idaho published its first "Blue Book," it included a list of several hundred leading Idahoans; Adams, who was at his influential zenith in the two decades before (and after) that book, didn't rate even a mention. Speculation: He arranged the omission.

Explaining the rankings of some of the people on this list is straightforward: They founded this, shaped that. Adams' achievements were done in conjunction with other people, working through other people, and many of them were behind the scenes – often *way* behind. But many of the results are visible enough.

The Idaho Statehouse has passed through its centennial, celebrated in part with a remodeling and also with extensive retelling of its history. One story not told was of how the Statehouse came close to not getting its two "wings" – where the legislative chambers are located – and what bit of legerdemain got it done.

The year was 1919, after completion of the central section of the Statehouse, which contained the executive offices, the Supreme Court, *and* was where the legislature met. The issue was whether to spend the large amount of money needed to build the wings, and the legislature was deeply divided on the idea – headed toward its rejection. Had it failed that session, the building might have been put off for many years, through the tight "economy bloc" years of the '20s, through the political battles of the '30s, maybe much longer.

During the 1919 legislative session the key to passage was a particular state senator, who could swing a group of undecided votes. Mid-session, the senator (a former bar owner) was upset, because the Ada County Sheriff's Office had raided his hotel room and, since prohibition was already in force in Idaho, seized his stash of alcohol. His angry frame of mind set him up for a "no" vote – but then stepped in a dapper, soft-spoken lobbyist from Rexburg. Join me tonight, he said, for dinner with the Boise Chamber of Commerce.

As part of the dinner's festivities, the senator's hosts presented him with his confiscated liquor, a new silver flask and a note of apology from the sheriff's office.

The lobbyist – Lloyd Adams, who had arranged it all – got the senator's vote, and the wings.

To gauge Adams' impact on Idaho, multiply that story by the scores, if not more.

Adams was born in Nephi, Utah, in 1885, then a hardscrabble Mormon town on the edge of the Salt Lake basin. Set to work at an early age, he started as a printer's devil at weekly newspapers in Utah, became a reporter, then in 1906 migrated north to an Idaho printing job at one of the weeklies (In those days even the smaller towns usually had more than one.) in St. Anthony. He was soon editing the paper in Sugar City, then took over the Rexburg *Standard*, which he would run until 1938. Rexburg was home for the rest of his life.

When he arrived in Idaho, Republican politics were in tumult, highly factious; Adams picked his side early on and stuck with it.

In the gubernatorial campaign of 1912 one of the big issues was the beating death of a juvenile inmate at the state "Industrial School" at St. Anthony. Adams, whose Republican paper was located on the scene, was central in developing that incident as an issue against incumbent Democratic governor James Hawley whose Republican opponent, John Haines, was tainted by allegations of corruption during his years in Boise city politics. When he beat Hawley by just 1,064 votes, the St. Anthony issue was thought to be a big factor. Adams leveraged his new influence, becoming a tight ally of Frank Gooding and John Thomas, the leaders and de facto founders of the modern Idaho Republican Party (and in part of its modern banking industry).

For many years, notably in the '20s, Adams virtually hand-picked governors and other key officials. He was a central engine behind election of at least a dozen governors overall, including the governor (Don Samuelson) who held the office at Adams' death.

Nor was his influence limited to Republican circles. He took care to do favors for (and ask favors from) Democrats as well. He counseled Democratic governor C. Ben Ross (whose policies he strongly influenced) and is said to have advised Democratic Gov. Charles Gossett in 1945 to resign so he would be appointed to the U.S. Senate. (A disastrous decision for Gossett and for Democrats, since Republicans won both the governorship and the Senate seat the next year. Adams is said to have been hiding out in the governor's coat closet when Gossett held the press conference announcing the appointment.)

On a practical level, Adams engineered the 1913 split-off of Madison County from Fremont County, and the early construction of the highway from Idaho Falls northeast to Yellowstone National Park, which allowed for much of the California traffic to and subsequent development of the west side of the park and of the West Yellowstone area (and the hugely popular tourist zone in Idaho southwest of the national park).

As a lobbyist, he cut deals that changed the governor's terms from two-year to four-year increments, and then from a one-term limitation to no limitation, and for creation of the Port of Lewiston.

Adams was a political man in every reasonable sense of the word, and his astonishingly full awareness of the possibilities and limitations of politics account for his place on this list. None of the conventional measures of visible influence account for it. He served in elective office just two years as a state senator. Asked periodically why he didn't run for governor, he would reply, "Because I don't want to be an ex-governor" – but the real reason was that, in most cases, the governorship would have marked a step down in influence.

His sense of politics was unmatched, and his personal skill in reading and working with people remarkable. On the occasion when Adams ran for the state Senate, he had developed rivals and enemies in the area, and they tried hard to take him down. One associate of Adams recalled that "on the Sunday before election day, [an organizer for his opponent, a high LDS church official] summoned 3,000 Saints to stake conference in the tabernacle to hear Brother Blake, his first councilor and Fremont County's fire-and-brimstone Isaiah, thunder: 'Day after tomorrow you go to the polls to vote for state senator from Madison County. On the one hand you have God's anointed, God's mouthpiece, God's humble servant; and on the other hand you have the clever, cunning hand of Satan, Lloyd Adams. Take your choice."

They chose Adams. And the word was that, for much of the first half of the twentieth century, Adams had a strong voice in the direction of how eastern Idaho Mormons should vote. Certainly, they hardly ever ran counter to the directions he was pursuing.

He was the most effective lobbyist and political organizer Idaho has ever had. But for Lloyd Adams, Idaho might be more bipartisan instead of solidly Republican. But for Adams, Yellowstone Park might have developed very differently and been a smaller, more remote attraction with little link to Idaho; Lewiston might not have a port; the nature of banking, finance, and investment in Idaho (and the sizable yet localized capital base that allowed for formation of huge international corporations) might not have developed until much later, and in quite different ways. He literally made and unmade governors and senators, over a reach of decades, with reverberating impacts so extensive they're hard to contemplate. He became an insider with the skillful engineering (through a clever realignment of votes in the Upper Snake River Valley) of a narrow victory for a Republican governor in 1912, and remained a force to be reckoned with until his death in 1969.

He did it quietly. Most of the year, he worked out of his law office at Rexburg. During legislative sessions, he could be found only rarely at the Statehouse but often in room 124 of the Owyhee Hotel. (Adams once said he took the room on the night of the hotel's opening, and didn't relinquish it for decades.) He was said to be a legendarily skillful user of the telephone. He was also the first Idaho lobbyist to have multiple clients – a practice that is standard fare for many of today's lobbyists.

No one so powerfully turned, twisted, and affected Idaho so much over so many years as he did.

2 Elias Davidson PIERCE

1824-1897. Miner. Pierce. Buried: Pennville, Indiana, Hillside Cemetery.

Even for the mountain men and gold rush miners of the 1850s, the area that is now Idaho was awfully remote. There were settlements at Walla Walla to the west and in the Salt Lake area (and touching on the Idaho line at what is now Franklin) to the southeast, but no permanent American settlements in between. E.D. Pierce was the human trigger who changed that, turning Idaho history abruptly – not gradually – in a new direction.

What he did, and the discovery he made, was not a foregone conclusion, because in traveling east from Walla Walla with a party of 12, scouring mountainsides and creeks for signs of gold, Pierce was breaking the law and running considerable physical risk.

E.D. Pierce was born in Monaghan, Ireland, in 1824 and spent much of his life conquering new frontiers. He immigrated to Virginia at the age of 15, then moved on to Indiana where he became an attorney. After serving in the Mexican War, he traveled to California with the Forty-niners, and became an itinerant trader. He served in the California Legislature in 1852 and in 1854, became the first non-native person to summit Mount Shasta.

For his next frontier he moved to Walla Walla in Washington Territory, where he went from being lawmaker to lawbreaker.

He first visited the Nez Perce country in 1852-53 as an Indian trader. Convinced that he was near a great gold region, he returned in 1860. He broke a law barring trespass and entered the Nez Perce Indian Reservation on the North Fork of the Clearwater disguised as an Indian trader. Panning for gold on February 20, 1860, he made the first successful gold discovery in what would become Idaho.

In August he returned from Walla Walla with a group of twelve men. Sneaking onto the reservation, they spent six weeks prospecting before making a significant discovery on Oro Fino Creek on September 20, 1860.

The area would never be the same again. A second party arrived in December and founded a town they named Pierce. By the next summer, several thousand men were in the area seeking their fortunes. In the coming months they spread and discovered additional rich placers at Elk City and Florence. The steamboat *Idaho*, operating on the lower Columbia River, began ferrying supplies to the miners and the area was soon referred to as the Idaho mines.

Pierce traveled to the Territorial Legislature in Olympia, Washington to charter a wagon road from Walla Walla to the gold fields. In June 1861 the town of Pierce was named county seat for Shoshone County, and Shoshone County quickly became the most populous county in Washington Territory (making almost inevitable the soon-to-come split of Idaho from Washington). By June 1862 Idaho's first government building, the Pierce Courthouse, was chartered and by August 1862 construction was complete. That marked a starting point for law and order in Idaho.

Pierce himself was not much of a miner. He seems to have been more interested in discovering gold than in trying to make his fortune at it. He established a sawmill in Pierce in the spring of 1861, but soon left to try to find another major strike elsewhere. He moved back to California and in the early 1880s to become a pioneer fruit grower in the Napa Valley, but apparently made only a marginal living. In 1884 his brother-in-law sent money so he could return to Indiana. He died penniless on February 15, 1897, and is buried in an unmarked grave in Hillside Cemetery in Pennville, Indiana.

His original strike in Idaho resulted in the first influx of non-natives to Idaho and the creation of a supply town called Lewiston, which would become the territory's first capital.

From there came the mining strikes in the Florence area, south of present-day Grangeville, and miners explored from there into the Boise Basin, which rapidly saw the development of a small military post called Fort Boise into the commercial and governmental seat of Idaho. As the fever subsided there, miners moved on to the Owyhees and the Wood River Valley, and to other places.

Pierce's impact was like that of a firework igniting a series of cascading explosions. A great deal of Idaho history unfolded as it did because of Pierce's discovery.

3 | Ira Burton PERRINE

May 7, 1861 – October 2, 1943. Farmer, real estate developer. Twin Falls.

Ira "Burt" Perrine (who, like Lloyd Adams, was alive in 1935 but didn't make the cut for that year's state Blue Book) is best known now as namesake of the spectacular Highway 93 bridge over the Snake River Canyon at Twin Falls. He should be known as the man without whom that bridge would have little point. If south-central Idaho is indeed the Magic Valley, then Ira Perrine was the magician.

Born in Indiana into a family of 11 children, he determined to make his way in the frontier lands to the west. In 1884 he was drawn to the then-booming mining country in the Wood River Valley where he failed to find employment. After a series of "make-do" jobs, in the 1890s he tried to develop a cattle business to help supply the mines, but he found no grazing lands available nearby. No lands were available at all for almost 60 miles south, where he encountered the Snake River canyon.

What he did then was a bit magical indeed.

Perrine did not invent irrigation in Idaho. That credit goes to northern Idaho missionary Henry Spalding. Mormon farmers to the east also had developed a sophisticated water system decades before Perrine's efforts. Soon after, future governor William McConnell established one of the first irrigation projects in southwest Idaho, on the Payette River, but this too remained small in scope. No one in the Intermountain region had ever developed a massive irrigation system in the desert.

But that was Perrine's plan, and he had perfect timing. A businessman and a huckster, he saw opportunity in a political act: The Carey Act of 1894, which allotted big federal-backed benefits to anyone who would put desert land to irrigated use. The Carey Act gave western states vast acreages, provided they be irrigated; in the first decade after the act, more acres were secured in Idaho than in any other state, largely due to Perrine. About 60 percent of all Carey Act lands in the United States are in Idaho.

Deep in the Snake River canyon near what is now Twin Falls, Perrine started an orchard, found the soil fertile (albeit parched), and returned East to promote investment in irrigation projects. He envisioned a massive agricultural development in the empty south-central Idaho area, and started pulling in investors, many of them in Pennsylvania.

He got a boost from additional federal irrigation support in 1901 and 1902; by then investors were lined up and irrigation projects underway. In 1904, when many of them came into development, the support city of Twin Falls boomed overnight, becoming one of the nation's few farm boom towns. Together with a string of business allies who also left their names on Magic Valley towns and landmarks (Walter Filer, H.L. Hollister, Stanley Milner, Peter Kimberly, Frank Buhl), Perrine organized construction of the Milner Dam, the first major damming of the Snake River (which would have endless consequences); platted the Twin Falls townsite and organized the community; and set up the irrigation community that has sprawled over time throughout south central Idaho.

Perrine, as the leading figure in one of Idaho's larger communities until his death in 1943, played a public and political role in the state behind the scenes as well. Senator William Borah was an occasional visitor.

But Perrine is on this list for his role in practically creating a whole region of Idaho out of land which until then had been dismissed as uninhabitable. No one person can be truly considered the "father of Idaho," but Perrine can rightfully be called "the father of the Magic Valley."

4 William Horace CLAGETT

September 21, 1838 – August 3, 1901. Attorney. Murray. Buried: Spokane.

William H. Clagett, one of Idaho's founding fathers, could lay solid claim to the title, "Father of Idaho's Constitution."

He was born in Prince George's County, Maryland, in 1838. He moved with his family to Keokuk, Iowa, where he studied law and was admitted to the bar. At the age of 23, he moved to Carson City, Nevada, where he became close friends with Samuel L. Clemens [Mark Twain]. The adventures they shared were described in detail in the Twain book *Roughing It*.

Clagett specialized in mining law. He began his political career as a member of the Nevada legislature, before moving to Montana where he was elected as territorial delegate to Congress in 1870. For a non-voting territorial delegate, he had considerable success in Washington. His most notable achievement was sponsorship of legislation that created Yellowstone National Park.

From Montana he moved to Denver, then to the Black Hills of South Dakota, to Butte, Montana, and finally to Portland, Oregon. He was one of the first to arrive in northern Idaho when gold was discovered in the Coeur d'Alenes in 1883-84. He settled in Murray, over the mountain from Wallace, and established a law practice.

When Idaho's constitutional convention was called in 1889, it was held without any official authorization from Washington, D.C. The group that gathered in Boise to draft the constitution was acting on blind faith that Idaho was destined to soon become a state. To help steer them through the exercise, they elected Clagett as president of the convention.

Clagett not only presided over the convention, as George Washington had at the federal convention, but he also conceived and proposed the overall structure and sense of the constitution, just as James Madison had done at the federal level. In addition to that, he was the great orator at the convention, becoming known as the "Silver Tongued Orator of the West."

His oration wasn't simply for show. He pushed a number of specific and important elements, including methods of conducting jury trials and a strong statement on states rights. He was also the key mediator in developing the provision that barred Mormons from voting and serving on juries. He was a central figure on issues from public indebtedness in Idaho (a constitutional decision with vast ramifications), legislative apportionment, establishment of the courts and many more. He may also have been the main reason women's suffrage wasn't written into the Idaho constitution, as some delegates had proposed.

Ironically, in spite of his major role in creating the new state's government, he had no further political success in Idaho. When statehood came in 1890, he was unsuccessful in seeking election by the legislature to become one of Idaho's two United States senators. He also lost a second bid for the Senate. That ended his affiliation with the Republicans, after which he became an active proponent of the silver cause (promoting a silver-based currency), as a Populist. But after the mid-1890s, that counted for little.

He finally moved his law practice to Spokane, the urban headquarters of the Coeur d'Alene mining region. He died in Spokane on August 3, 1901, and is buried there.

In the big picture, Clagett's political losses hardly matter. He had more effect on the state of Idaho than anyone who ever served it in Congress.

5 Joe MARSHALL

April 3, 1874-January 1964. Farmer, food processor. Jerome.

With what single word is "Idaho" most associated? Nationwide, maybe worldwide, the obvious answer is "potato."

What's less well known is that this simple fact, a fact take for granted in Idaho, did not develop gradually and was in no sense inevitable. It was the direct result of a shrewd crusade by one man: Joe Marshall, a man who spotted and exploited an opportunity no one else saw.

A native of Ohio and like so many other influential early-day Idahoans a native Midwesterner, Marshall was born into a poor farm family; one early memory was of snow puffing through the walls of his family's cabin. He bounced across the West around the turn of the century, looking for opportunity, before settling in the Magic Valley in the Jerome area, in the wake of the Carey Act irrigation development there.

In those days Marshall was one of many young farmers, and like many others in this newly-watered land he grew potatoes. And like the others, he was dissatisfied with the low prices he got when he shipped spuds by rail to Chicago, the big commodity center. What set him aside was the uncommon thing he did about it.

Marshall had observed that many of the Idaho potatoes were, in several respects, superior, because of soil, growing conditions and other factors, to some of the other potatoes from across the West. The Idaho Potato Commission describes the superiority this way: "Idaho grown potatoes have a high solids content, so there's more potato and less water," and lead to a more attractive product when prepared.

But he also saw that any inherent advantage was lost in shipping: The Idaho product was tossed into shipments along with those from other regions. So, rather than work through the commodity wholesalers, he started in 1917 trying to retail potatoes, (mostly under his Blue Diamond label, which is still widespread) as special, premium potatoes. He persuaded several chains of restaurants to carry them, then persuaded grocery stores as well when he packaged them in consumer-friendly bags.

He was rewarded with premium prices for his potatoes, and he prospered. Throughout, he pushed – hard – the idea that Idaho's were superior potatoes.

There matters might have stood except for the massive agricultural price collapse after World War I. Farmers were stretched to the limit, and farm lenders were desperate. Several key Idaho lenders asked Marshall to take over the business and marketing activities of many – certainly more than 100, possibly 200 – farms across southern Idaho, as far away as Aberdeen. He did, and used the chance to impose his own approach on all of them, in effect building a comprehensive Idaho potato industry among scores of Idaho farmers simultaneously. A naturally gifted promoter, Marshall used his control over this abruptly increased volume of potatoes to push nationally the idea of the wonderful Idaho potato.

That crusade has had huge impacts on Idaho ever since, only beginning with the state's identification with the vegetable in the minds of ... most of the world. Marshall's promotional activity made possible the growth and development of the J.R. Simplot Company, for by World War II even the U.S. military (Simplot's first big customer) was primed for the idea of relying on Idaho potatoes.

Marshall's activities led to the massive food-processing industry in southern Idaho, and locked in place Idaho agriculture as a prosperous endeavor for many years.

6 James AILSHIE

June 19, 1868 – May 27, 1947. Attorney. Supreme Court Justice. Boise.

If William Clagett was Idaho's James Madison, then James Ailshie was its John Marshall. No one did more to establish Idaho's state court system and its sense of jurisprudence, not only in form but in substance as well.

The decade after statehood found Ailshie a lawyer, practicing in the Grangeville area. He decided to run for justice on the Idaho Supreme Court in 1902, at a time when that office was both highly partisan and usually contested. Ailshie was a well-connected Republican, and his political timing was good.

His years of service on the Supreme Court set two records that still stand. No one else has served in two separate runs (from 1903-14 and 1935-47), or across such a lengthy period (though a few have served longer in total years).

He is not on this list for reasons of longevity, though. Ailshie was a legal pioneer who took a lead role on many of the most important decisions of the young court, and helped establish it as a force to be reckoned with.

One report notes: "During his 24 years on the bench about two-thirds of the state constitution was tested before the court. He authored more than 700 opinions, including *The State vs. Moyer, Haywood and Pettibone* (April 14, 1906)."

Possibly the single most important thing he did – and the available records suggest that he was the justice most responsible – was the shrewd legal argument (in *Dudley Toncray v. Alfred Budge*) that undermined and tossed out the Idaho Constitution ban, and earlier territorial law, prohibiting voting by Mormons. It drew a sharp distinction between religious beliefs and practices that has held up since.

In the decision, the court said, "Now, celestial and patriarchal marriages, to be participated in in the next world, cannot be crimes here and in this life under a civil and man-made government; but, whenever they are practiced, in this present life, to the extent of more than one at a time, they become bigamous or polygamous, and are prohibited by the organic law of the state. It therefore clearly appears that the [constitutional] convention itself was guarding against acts and practices and teachings, and not against beliefs."

Since then, Mormons have become a major part of Idaho's civic life.

He played important roles in establishing the limits of power of Idaho government in the area of eminent domain (in *Washington Water Power. v. Waters*) and elsewhere. He was also something of a judicial reformer, pushing through some reforms early in the century, and later set the stage for developing of a comprehensive set of court rules of procedure.

7 Thomas E. ROACH

- June 1983. Utility executive. Boise.

No business in Idaho has had more to do with making Idaho the way it is, than Idaho Power Company; during its peak of clout, one wag suggested that it was Idaho state's namesake. And no one of Idaho Power's leaders over its century of existence has influenced its growth – and the state's – more than Tom Roach.

Outside of Idaho Power, Roach probably is little remembered, and unlike many of the people on this list he did not change the basic direction of the state. But his extension of one of the most important trends around was so important and so sweeping that his actions clearly were among the most central of any Idahoan's on the future of the state.

Roach, a veteran company man, was preceded as president and chairman of Idaho Power by Clifford J. Strike. The C.J. Strike Dam is named after him, and for good reason; Strike took as a goal extending the hydropower base on which Idaho Power was founded a third of a century earlier. When Roach took over in 1948 (his eventual control of the corporation, for two decades, lasted longer than anyone's before or since) he adopted Strike's general direction in expanding hydropower capabilities and pushed hard, very hard.

Four basic points should be made about the results of Roach's efforts.

First, the three Hells Canyon Dams (Brownlee, Oxbow, and Hells Canyon) were built on the Snake River, directly as a result of Roach's work. This was no foregone conclusion; powerful forces fought for a single (high) federal dam, or (to a lesser extent) for no dam at all. The existence of those dams can be attributed mostly to Roach and secondarily to his political ally, Governor Len Jordan.

Second, those dams were what allowed Idaho Power to grow. It unleashed the corporation, which within a decade of their construction became the largest hydro-based private utility in the country. A great deal of the development of Idaho in the sixties and seventies was closely related to that development.

Third, the fact that these were private dams and not federal in ownership – like the Grand Coulee and other massive Columbia River system dams – probably had a significant effect on the way Idahoans (as opposed to Washingtonians and Oregonians) think about the federal government, and its relationship to business.

Fourth, the construction of those dams and others launched a cascading series of events that led inexorably to the Swan Falls decision by the Idaho Supreme Court, and later to the Snake River Basin Adjudication, which as this book is written is in the process of assigning water rights to 87 percent of Idaho.

Roach, in other words, was the one Idaho Power president who had immense influence far beyond the service area of his utility.

8 Thomas RICKS

July 21, 1828 – September 28, 1901. Pioneer leader. Rexburg.

When Mormon pioneers first came to Idaho, in Franklin in 1860, they were simply extending, by increments, their settlements in Utah. (Indeed those first Franklin settlers actually thought they were still in Utah – a debate that wasn't resolved until a survey in the 1870s made clear the actual border.) The southern parts of what are now Franklin, Bear Lake, and Cassia counties were the first settled by immigrants from Utah.

Continued movement north, however, seemed problematic.

An earlier attempt by the church to plant a group well to the north, near Salmon at a place called Fort Lemhi, ended in disaster when Indian tribes attacked, and possible attacks remained a concern in many areas through the 1860s and 1870s. At the same time, non-Mormons were beginning to develop their own communities in places like Pocatello and Eagle Rock (now Idaho Falls), and many of these settlers were extremely hostile to the Mormons. By 1880 the northern migration of Utahns, and the substantial growth of the church in southern Idaho, might have been choked.

That it was not, and that almost all of populated Eastern Idaho today is heavily Mormon in population, is attributable in largest part to one man: Thomas Ricks, the namesake and founder of both Rexburg and Ricks College.

To be sure, the whole thing wasn't Ricks's idea. A faithful member of the church, he had undertaken various difficult tasks before and did not balk when William Preston, the president of the

Cache Valley stake, asked him to go where no Mormon leader had successfully gone before, far to the north to establish a settlement.

In 1883 Ricks took about a dozen settlers with him to what became Rexburg (the name derived from a Latinization of Ricks); within a couple of years, the population was zooming up toward 1,000, and the new community was set in place. An academy was established there, so LDS children could attend school in peace in that time of vicious anti-Mormon bigotry; its successor Ricks College – renamed in 1998 as Brigham Young University-Idaho – became the largest private college in Idaho, so popular among LDS students that an attendance cap was ultimately set.

Thomas Ricks' descendants (including a recent state senator and lieutenant governor, Mark Ricks) have been locally prominent in the century since.

Apart from Ira Perrine, no one person has had greater direct impact on a large region of Idaho than Thomas Ricks. In fact, some current economists believe that, if the federal government were to close its national laboratory in Idaho Falls, Rexburg and Madison County would become the economic center of eastern Idaho.

9 Fred T. DUBOIS

May 29, 1851 – February 14, 1930. Marshal. U.S. Senator. Blackfoot. Buried: Blackfoot.

In an era full of anti-Mormon politicians, Fred T. Dubois stood out as a leader of the pack.

More than that, he was as central a figure as any in the development of Idaho state, experienced great short-term success and even greater long-term failure, and still emerges as one of the key people in Idaho history.

His short-term success and long-term failure concerned the Idaho Mormons, whose very existence in the state he would, presumably, have liked to seen eradicated. (Though he was by no means alone; he received strong encouragement and support from territorial governor John Neil, among others.)

Illinois native Dubois grew up in Springfield. His father was a close friend of Abraham and Mary Lincoln, accompanying both Lincolns on the train ride to Washington on Lincoln's way to his inauguration as president and returning with his body and Mary Lincoln after his assassination. Fred Dubois came to Idaho as a cowboy and emerged into territory-wide visibility as a U.S. marshal. Whether his antagonism toward Mormons derived from personal beliefs or political ambition is unclear, but the politics were crystalline: Dubois was a Republican, and most Mormons then were Democrats. Dubois devised a way to begin mass convictions of Mormons on polygamy charges by excluding them from juries, then whipping up gentile opposition. These activities made Dubois a rising star in Republican circles.

Dubois was a successful persecutor. But long term, over his bitter objections – which led in the new century to his becoming a Democrat, and in turn encouraging many Mormons to turn Republican – Idaho turned away from anti-Mormonism.

He is ranked high on this list mainly because of his purely political and organizational achievements.

The Republican Party in Idaho was swept up in faction fights for most of the 1880s, one of the reasons for national GOP skepticism about admitting Idaho as a state. Dubois was a player in these fights for a while from his Blackfoot-area base, but by 1883 was sitting most of them out, quietly building personal organization support for himself around the territory.

When the political bloodletting eased in Boise, with both a "ring" and an alternate "anti-Mormon" faction badly beaten, Dubois stepped in, forced the two sides to come to terms, took over and reorganized the GOP organization, and got himself elected as territorial delegate to Congress.

He was Idaho's last territorial delegate, successful in his major mission in Washington: Pushing Idaho through to statehood. The ardent Republican had little luck at first, during the Democratic Cleveland administration, though he built groundwork for statehood by working closely with Democratic territorial governor Edward Stevenson. When Republican Benjamin Harrison became president in 1889, Dubois was well-positioned to exert his influence, and rammed statehood through.

That it came when it did, in the form it did, is due more to him than to anyone else. On July 3, 1890, he was the only witness when President Benjamin Harrison signed the Idaho statehood bill.

Dubois remained influential in early statehood. He won a term in the U.S. Senate in 1900, by which time he had switched parties (having lost control of the Republicans around the time of statehood) to become a Democrat. Idaho's Republican legislature replaced him, after the 1906 election, with Republican William E. Borah.

After that, Dubois stayed in Washington D.C. the rest of his life, becoming periodically involved in Democratic politics but never again with Idaho matters. He was, however, buried in Blackfoot.

His impact in Idaho far outstripped his effect in Washington. In the U.S. Senate, his greatest legacy may have been his successful effort to have Senate bean soup made a permanent part of the menu in the Senate restaurant.

10 WETXUWIIS

17?-18?. Nez Perce tribal member. Weippe.

In September 1805 the exploring party led by Meriwether Lewis and William Clark, exhausted and sickly, staggered onto the Weippe Prairie and encountered Idaho's first, and one of its most significant, historical forks in the road. They encountered it in the persons of a group of natives of the area, Ni Mii Pu, more commonly now known as Nez Perce.

The Ni Mii Pu men who bumped into Lewis, Clark, and the others in their expedition were unsure what to do about them. Stories of what happened when Europeans encountered natives may have circulated already, and a number of tribal members thought the best thing to do would be to slaughter them.

It would not have been difficult. Lewis was so ill he could hardly travel, Clark had just broken his hip after being thrown from his horse, and others in the party were no better off. Even without an attack, their odds of reaching the Pacific, or home, were not great at that point.

The tribal members returned to their camp and the larger group discussed the issue. We have no minutes of the discussion, but Nez Perce tradition has long held that the decisive argument came from an old woman named Wetxuwiis. We know little about her, but the tradition holds that many years before, she had been captured by other tribes and taken many miles to the east. A group of whites helped her escape and return home, she said, and now this group should be given the same assistance.

That was what happened. Oblivious to the close call, the Lewis and Clark party were invited to the village, fed, treated for various ailments, and given practical advice on survival in the region – how to build more sturdy boats, for example, and how to use wood and build fires more efficiently. And they were sent on their way with directions to the Pacific.

But suppose Wetxiwiis, or someone like her, had not taken up the travelers' cause? Suppose Lewis and Clark had simply, mysteriously, vanished somewhere in the Pacific Northwest?

The return of Lewis and Clark caused a sensation in the new United States, and led to a string of developments toward the Pacific, but those might have been crucially delayed. The founding of Astoria by an American fur company in 1811 (near the Lewis and Clark Pacific camp site) might not have happened but for the reports from the expedition. Meanwhile, the British from Canada were working the area steadily through the Hudson's Bay Company. It's not a reach to suggest that what's now Idaho, and points west, might today be part of Canada if Lewis and Clark had not returned.

The history of what is now Idaho might have been altogether different but for a woman who, one September evening, counseled mercy rather than war.

11 John R. SIMPLOT

January 9, 1909 – May 25, 2008. Business owner. Boise. Buried: Boise, Morris Hill Cemetery.

It'd be hard to nail down conclusively, but the J.R. Simplot Co., together with the companies it controls or founded, likely has employed more people for more years than any other private sector employer in Idaho, ever.

J.R. Simplot the person, however, is a big figure in Idaho history for more reasons than just paychecks. He created, built and ran the largest privately-owned (as opposed to publicly traded) business in Idaho, which means he had more direct control over it than did the executives of many other large Idaho-founded, but publicly traded, corporations had over theirs. Those other executives have had to work within corporate frameworks, and in the case of some who extended their activities outside the norm (such as Robert Hansberger at Boise Cascade), they often find themselves looking for employment elsewhere. Simplot had no such constraints. He had both the latitude to throw his weight around, and the willingness to do it, often experimenting and taking chances. Idaho is a lot different from what it would have been without him.

An eighth grade dropout in the tiny burg of Declo, Simplot early on envisioned business opportunities where others missed them. He also took risks. In 1929 he got ownership of a potato sorter, and leveraged that into a fast-growing potato distribution business, adding onions over the next decade. In 1940 he happened onto a buyer of dehydrated onions who was dissatisfied with the service he'd been getting from another supplier. Simplot immediately offered the buyer a better deal, which was accepted; then, Simplot had to figure out how to do what he'd just promised. But, as on many other occasions, he did.

Potato processing had never been a foundation of a truly big business but Simplot saw a string of opportunities, starting with the Army's need for dehydrated potatoes in World War II and McDonald's need a decade later for French fries, and exploited those needs brilliantly.

Few businesses contained the diversity of Simplot's operations prior to him stepping away from active management: Seeds, fertilizer, livestock, row crops, food processing, mining, and table-ready food products are only part of the picture.

Simplot is an international business, but its impact has always been heaviest in Idaho. Not content with just running his own business, J.R. bought plenty of others, mainly ag-related in some fashion, in the state. He also helped launch the largest single private employer in the Boise area – Micron Technology – and for years played a big role in its development.

Simplot ranks lower on this list than another businessman in a similar line of business: Joe Marshall, who in effect "created" the Idaho potato. The foundation of Simplot's business (potato processing) was dependent on and grew out of Marshall's work.

That's no denigration of Simplot's importance in Idaho though. His reach is such that the effects of his business activities are likely to be important across Idaho for decades at least.

12 William DEARY

1853 - May 7, 1913. Timber company executive. Potlatch.

The industrial giant/robber baron figure behind the Idaho timber industry was Frederick Weyerhaeuser, a magnate from St. Paul, Minnesota, who visited Idaho for nine days in 1900 and thought the forests in the northern part of the state (then in pre-National Forest status, and available for acquisition) would make a good timber supply. A year later, he dispatched agents to Idaho to check out the possibilities and, maybe, start building a business. Massive land purchases followed. Weyerhaeuser is clearly a significant figure, therefore, in Idaho history, in that he started the ball rolling toward development of what became northern Idaho's main economic base for most of the twentieth century (and will be noted as such later in this list). His role, however, was that of bankroller and initial motivator of the effort; he did not direct it or shape it locally and he was not present in Idaho to push it. His initial efforts easily could have come to nothing.

That they did come to something – quite a lot, in fact – is due largely to William Deary.

Born on Allumette Island in Quebec, Deary spent years as a lumberman in Ontario. He got into the timber business himself after a time, eventually starting a timber company with a partner from Wisconsin. That got him into the world of major timber company owners, especially Weyerhaeuser, for whom he started spearheading major projects.

Deary came to Idaho in 1901 on a timber-buying mission, and buy he did: The largest chunk of what is now private timber lands in Northern Idaho is land Deary picked out and bought. He established the Potlatch Lumber Company, and became its first general manager; the company was the dominant force in northern Idaho timber production for many years. Potlatch (and, recently, its successors) have been the largest single private employer in north-central Idaho most of the last century.

He's also one of the few people on this list who could legitimately be said to have created outright an entire Idaho city: That of Potlatch, in northern Latah County, which was for many years a purely company town. (His own namesake is the town of Deary, not far away.)

Deary would rank higher on this list if he were the initial force and entrepreneur behind the development of northern Idaho. In fact, he was a hired hand carrying out orders. But the results of his efforts, and specific decisions and instructions, were so momentous for such a large region that he still merits a key spot.

13 William BUDGE

May 1, 1828 – March 1, 1919. LDS Church leader. Paris.

Probably no single person did more to extend the Church of Jesus Christ of Latter-day Saints into Idaho than Thomas Ricks, but probably no one person did more to develop its content, structure, and place in Idaho society, during the state's initial formative period, than William Budge.

He spent much of his life far from Idaho. A native of Lanark, Scotland, he converted to the LDS Church at 20 and for a decade after that served as a missionary, mainly in Great Britain but on expeditions around Europe as well. In 1860 he moved to Utah, where he was ordained a bishop by Brigham Young. Soon after he was sent north to Bear Lake Stake, based at Paris in Idaho's Bear Lake County, which had been founded recently by Charles Rich. In 1870 Budge was named stake president. He held that position, according to church records, until 1906.

In that place and time, it was a highly important role. While Mormons were beginning to spread out around eastern Idaho, they remained concentrated nearly until the new century in the southeastern corner of the state – Ricks would not found Rexburg until 1883 – and Bear Lake was the one overwhelmingly Mormon county in Idaho until the 1890s. Bear Lake was the first Idaho stake, and although by 1890 there were four more, Budge's seniority and high standing in the church made him, as one historian wrote, the church's "major agent in Idaho."

In a comprehensive 1977 article on the Mormon vote, historian E. Leo Lyman noted that Bear Lake County in particular "functioned almost as a theocracy, with government officials largely ratifying and administering decisions actually made by President William Budge and other priesthood leaders of the Bear Lake Stake, who presided over the same geographic area that the county included."

The effects were wide-ranging, but perhaps most dramatic in Idaho politics. Budge was the man most central in moving Idaho's Mormon community from overwhelming Democratic to overwhelming Republican support. Many Republicans nationally had been fiercely anti-Mormon, while Democrats were more divided on whether to accept them or not, a division point important in Idaho territorial politics. Budge led the Idaho Mormon community through strong support for Democrats in the 1870s (at a time when Mormons in Wyoming were strongly Republican), but he noted that Democrats only partially reciprocated. In an 1886 letter to Idaho Democratic leaders he described the Republicans as vampires and reminded them that "the Mormon vote [could be] counted on as solid," but: "If you want the support of the Mormon voters in this political crisis, you must be prepared to stand by them as they stand by you. There must be no flinching, no faltering, no cowardice."

At the Democratic convention that year, though, all three were on display, as congressional nominee John Hailey (who had won office earlier on the strength of Mormon votes) denounced the church, and Mormon delegates were kicked out of the meeting.

That started a transition, under Budge's supervision, away from the Democrats. He did not give up on them immediately, but he surely was one of a group of church leaders who convened in July 1890 at Salt Lake City to discuss politics. While Wyoming Mormons were advised to vote Republican, those in Idaho were told to stop cooperation with that state's Democratic party. The Bear Lake County newspaper, once called the *Democrat*, was renamed the *Southern Idaho Independent*. Over the next few years, Budge began meeting with Republicans, and developed friendly relations with them. And when he was elected to one term in the Idaho Senate in 1898, he ran as a Republican – surely a powerful signal in the region, and the launch of a long-running trend.

Among the people who took personal actions to transform Idaho in important ways, William Budge must surely rank high.

14 Frank CHURCH

July 25, 1924 – April 7, 1984. Attorney. U.S. Senator. Boise. Buried: Boise, Morris Hill Cemetery.

Possibly the two best-known names in national politics that Idaho produced, as well as the only two who ran for president on a major party ballot, are William Borah and Frank Church. The comparisons between them are striking. Both served many years in the Senate (Borah five terms, Church four); both chaired the Senate Foreign Relations Committee; both were nationally and even internationally prominent; both exhibited (in different ways) some isolationist tendencies (a point not to be pushed too far); both were wonderful orators; both married daughters of Idaho governors; both exhibited the reserve and dignity thought to be Senator-like; both were genuine forces in the Senate; both conflicted with presidents of their own party, and with organizationally dominant leaders of their own party in Idaho ... and on and on.

Church, for that matter, was profoundly influenced by Borah and based his ambitions for the Senate, for the presidency, and for the Foreign Relations Committee in part on Borah's example.

A list of the most influential U.S. senators nationally would rank them differently, with Borah perhaps a bit higher. On this list of influence in Idaho, however, the distinction is plain: Church obviously is the bigger presence, Borah a shadow by comparison.

Why?

First, Church was far more involved with Idaho than Borah.

Church was an Idaho native with Idaho roots. (His grandfather moved to Idaho in territorial days to the Boise Basin mining district.)

An attorney in Boise, he became one of the leaders of the then-thin Idaho Democratic organization in Ada County, ran for the legislature in 1952 and lost. The idea of running for the U.S. Senate just four years later seemed a very long shot, but political and personal appeal and a string of good fortune won his election that year, ousting a Republican incumbent. That Republican, Herman Welker, was the last Republican defeated for re-election to the Senate in Idaho, and Church himself eventually the last senator of either party defeated for the job.

Church became one of the more visible senators shortly after his arrival, involved with passage of the 1957 civil rights act and, not long after, active in foreign affairs as well. His eventual protests against the Vietnam conflict would make him a nationally recognized figure. But not all of this was popular in Idaho, and his Vietnam stance led to an abortive recall attempt back home. Still, he was re-elected to the Senate in 1962, by a landslide in 1968 and by a smaller margin in 1974. Controversy over a range of efforts, from his investigation of the CIA to support of the 1978 Panama Canal treaties, and his presidential run in 1976, caught up with Church in 1980 when he narrowly lost his bid for a fifth term in the face of the Reagan landslide.

But Church's political base never was as broad or secure as Borah's. The pressure was on him to bring home the bacon, and he did. He was centrally involved in designation of many of Idaho's recreation and wilderness areas. He pushed through funding for U.S. Highway 12, the road connecting Lewiston with Missoula (an important roadway nonexistent until the sixties). He was an important benefactor of the Idaho National Engineering Laboratory in the sixties, a critical time when it might otherwise have been scaled back because of its aging nuclear plants. He played important roles in the Hells Canyon and wilderness debates. (Including his name on Idaho's largest wilderness area, with support from the state's Republican congressional delegation, was apt.) His ongoing close ties to Idaho throughout his Senate years was, among other things, a political necessity.

Because of those effects, Church was one of the most important figures in Idaho political history.

He remade the Idaho Democratic Party: What it became for the next three decades grew directly out of Church's activities in the sixties.

Previously, it had been fairly tightly-organized, based around socially-conservative labor-union structures that supported the party generally. Early on, Church realized that he needed his own organization, one more specifically loyal to him, if he were to survive. In 1966, he and the party organization clashed over the Democratic replacement nominee for governor (Church backed Cecil Andrus), and Church's side prevailed; the conservative Democratic organization wilted and died, and many of its leading members became Republicans. The Democratic Party in Idaho increasingly became the Church and Andrus fan club, which served those two major officials well but left the party in a disastrous state after both left the public scene. Borah, by contrast, had scant involvement over the years with the Idaho Republican Party once he was elected to the Senate.

Today, Idahoans are directly affected by a myriad of Church-supported efforts: Employment at the Idaho National Laboratory, the Sawtooth National Recreation Area, wilderness areas, wild and scenic rivers, and – nationally – the annual cost-of-living increase for Social Security recipients. No single elected official in modern times has had a greater impact on Idaho than Frank Church.

15 Frank FENN

September 11, 1853 – June 19, 1927. Attorney. Mount Idaho. Buried: Kooskia, Pine Grove Cemetery.

In 1905, with strong support from President Theodore Roosevelt, Congress passed legislation creating the U.S. Forest Service. A lot of invention had to follow that action. Policing the use of federal lands was a relatively new activity. The United States, and especially the West, had been settled largely by people desiring to develop federally-owned land and water and convert them to private use by farming, mining, logging, and other efforts. What should be done about land designated specifically as public?

Imagine the challenges faced by Frank Fenn when he was appointed superintendent of all federal forest reserves in Idaho. Suddenly people were going to be told – for the first time – what they could and could not do on large tracts of federal land.

He at least had good grounding in Idaho.

The Fenns were true Idaho pioneers. They moved from California to Florence in 1862, the year before Idaho became a territory. Frank's father, Stephen, mined and ran a store in Florence. He was elected to the second session of the territorial legislature and served four terms, then represented Idaho as its territorial delegate to congress from 1875-79.

Frank was one of seven students who attended Idaho's first public school and, in 1869 received an appointment to the U.S. Naval Academy, which he left in 1872 without graduating. When he returned to Idaho, he taught and operated a ranch. In 1886 Fenn was elected to the territorial legislature from Idaho County, and in 1890 he was elected to the first session of the state legislature, where he served as Speaker of the House. Then, in 1891, he was appointed chief clerk of the newly formed State Land Board. In 1896 he left the Land Board and was again elected to the legislature, this time from Ada County. He also read law and was admitted to the bar in 1897. In 1898 he volunteered for service in the Spanish-American War. He served in the Philippines and was discharged in 1899 as a major. From then on he was referred to in Idaho as Major Fenn.

Fenn returned to Boise, practiced law, and became chairman of the state Republican Central Committee. In 1901 he was appointed superintendent of all federal forest reserves in Idaho. In 1904, the year before the Forest Service was created, the forest reserves were reorganized and Fenn was put in charge of the Boise and Payette forest reserves where he became absorbed in solving grazing disputes with ranchers, who were accustomed to free-range grazing on federal lands.

In 1908 he became the first forest supervisor of the Clearwater National Forest, and, in 1911 supervisor of the newly formed Selway National Forest. In 1914, he was named chief of lands in the regional office of the Forest Service in Missoula.

These were formative years in the development and administration of policies governing the use of both state and federal lands. It was also a time when the use of public lands was critical to continuing the growth of Idaho's economy, since rural areas held most of the state's population and commerce. Major Fenn was there at the beginning and played perhaps a greater role than any other Idahoan in both developing and enforcing those policies. Today central Idaho is filled with features named for Frank Fenn and his family. Fenn Ranger Station and Major Fenn Picnic Area on the Lochsa are named for Frank Fenn, as is Fenn Peak, the highest peak in the Selway Crags. Florence Lake is named for his wife. Lloyd Lake is named for his son, while Rhoda Creek is named for his daughter. The town of Fenn, near Grangeville, originally named Tharp, is named after Stephen Fenn.

16 Cecil D. ANDRUS

August 25, 1931 - . Logger. Businessman/consultant. Governor. Secretary of the Interior. Boise.

If the logical question for some (often lesser-known) people on this list is, "why are they on this list or ranked so high?," then in Cece Andrus' case it has to be the reverse: Many people might expect a higher ranking.

If this list reflected sheer force of will and power exerted over a long time, affecting lots of people, he surely would rank higher. He was governor of Idaho longer than anyone else, the first Idaho resident ever to serve in the Cabinet—and at that in a position (Interior) to affect Idaho profoundly. At no point was he a mere caretaker: Andrus was a strong, forceful, and highly capable and effective leader throughout.

But this list has little to do with any of that: It has to do with people who changed Idaho in basic, fundamental ways. Most of the people relatively high in this list wrenched Idaho in some radical new direction it would not have taken without them. That is less true of Andrus than of the people ranking higher.

An Oregon native, he came to Orofino to run a small logging operation his father had purchased. A few years later, he was in the state Senate, and by the end of his third term he was a leader in the new moderate wing of the Senate Democratic caucus. In 1966, he managed to lose twice in runs for governor, first losing the primary election and then, after the nominee died in a plane crash and Andrus was appointed to replace him, the general election.

Andrus did win the governorship four years later, was re-elected in a landslide in 1974, and was named Secretary of the Interior in 1977 in the Jimmy Carter administration. After Carter left office in 1981, he returned to Idaho and was elected to two more gubernatorial terms (in 1986 and 1990), setting a record for gubernatorial elections and longevity. He, with John Evans, kept the governorship in Democratic hands for an unusual 24 years. He has been a highly visible figure in the state since.

One of Andrus' greatest impacts may be psychological: He added in 1970 a new dimension to the way Idahoans think about their state, when he campaigned in part on "quality of life" as an important ideological consideration. The specific issue, the concrete point at stake, was the prospective development of the White Cloud Mountains for mining purposes (which Andrus opposed and then-governor Don Samuelson supported), but his stance on that environmental issue would mislead Democrats and Republicans both for a quarter-century. Andrus never was a radical environmentalist – he had been a logger by profession once, after all – but actually tended to be moderate on the issue. His '90s support of expansion of the Mountain Home Air Force Base training range, which many environmentalists bitterly opposed, was not the betrayal they alleged because it was in keeping with his general views.

Andrus was very much in favor of economic development, as he proved strikingly in his last two terms. He merely suggested that "quality of life" translated to more than just jobs and profits. He was a business developer in his first terms as well, providing one of the key sales pitches that brought Hewlett Packard to Boise (a move that became a critical turning point for southwestern Idaho). "Quality of life" was an argument that sold convincingly to Idahoans, and which has fenced in what might have been more ambitious agendas in the area by conservative Republicans.

Andrus himself often said that his biggest efforts went into education. School-related issues were his prompt for running for the legislature in 1960, and they were as big an issue in his first winning campaign in 1970 as quality of life. The substantial expansion of education budgets and activities (including public kindergartens) in

Idaho since 1970 can be attributed to a substantial degree to Andrus' efforts.

And there was much more, scattered.

He pushed for a statewide local planning and zoning law, and he was an important booster of Idaho's economy in the mid-'80s, when it badly needed a good booster. He fought against the unlimited shipments of nuclear waste into eastern Idaho. He was the centerpiece, the psychological anchor, of the Idaho Democratic Party from 1980 until his retirement from the governorship in early 1995, and he played a key role (along with Frank Church) in dismantling an earlier party organization, replacing it with one of their own.

As Interior Secretary, he took several actions of import related to Idaho, notably expansion of the Snake River Birds of Prey National Conservation area.

In the end, Cecil Andrus probably draws greater continuing respect from a broader group of Idahoans than anyone else on this list. His popularity seems to have grown since he left office in 1995.

17 Edward STEVENSON

June 15, 1831 – July 6, 1895. Attorney and miner. Territorial governor. Grimes Pass. Buried: Boise, Pioneer Cemetery.

How's this for a scenario: Southern Idaho divided between Utah and Nevada, and northern Idaho comprising the eastern part of Washington state.

Few Idahoans today know how close that came to becoming reality: For a time in the 1880s, it was much more than just loose northern secessionist talk.

Nevada then had been a state since the Civil War, but it was a state in a world of hurt. The "rotten borough" had not really qualified for state status at its time of admission, and won that status only because of its rich mining reserves and the fact that the additional two votes in the U.S. Senate that were badly needed by Republicans during the Civil War. By the 1880s, with the mines in collapse and no other economic base in sight, Nevada was spiraling downward. Many people, there and elsewhere, thought the answer was to add territory to it. But California to the west already was a state, and so was Oregon to the north, and Utah had been extracted from Nevada because of pressure against admitting a Mormon state to the Union. That left the Idaho territory to the north. One scenario had it that Utah would pull in some of the eastern Idaho territory that already had a significant Mormon population.

Meanwhile, northern Idahoans were still, after a quarter-century, angry about their shotgun marriage to the south, and what appears to have been a clear majority wanted to join with Washington. The Nevada interests in Congress were willing to help them cut a deal. Such a deal actually passed both houses of Congress in 1887 and arrived at the desk of President Grover Cleveland. Idaho was one signature away from being wiped out of existence.

That is why Edward Stevenson is on this list.

Stevenson was a Cleveland appointee, like the president a Democrat, and also the first Idaho territorial resident to be appointed governor. There is evidence that Cleveland might have signed the bill but for Stevenson's telegraphed, and strongly worded, intervention. Odds are, there would be no Idaho today but for him.

Stevenson was born June 15, 1831, in Lowville, New York, into one of America's great political families. His brother, Charles, was governor of Nevada; his half-brother John became the first speaker of the Legislative Assembly of Ontario; and his cousin Adlai became Vice President of the United States. Adlai's grandson Adlai II would be elected governor of Illinois and twice nominated for President (1952 and 1956). Adlai III would be elected U.S. Senator from Illinois.

Stevenson left home at age 18 and arrived in California in 1849 to participate in the gold rush. He was elected to the California legislature and served two terms, then went to work as an Indian agent (during which time Indians killed his wife and three children). He was then elected to two more terms in the legislature and became speaker pro tempore. He remarried and had one son.

In 1863 the Stevensons moved to Idaho Territory, where they settled in the Boise Basin and Edward became involved in mining. He was elected in 1866 to the Territorial Council (the territorial equivalent of the state Senate); in 1874 he ran for the territorial House and became Speaker of the House. Two years later he was again elected to the Territorial Council. After that term, he was elected to the Boise County Commission; he read law, was admitted to the bar, and in 1882 moved to the Payette area and became a farmer.

In the 1880s a national movement was under way to discourage appointment of non-residents as territorial governors, and instead to seek out qualified residents. Based on the recommendation of Territorial Delegate John Hailey, President Cleveland nominated

Stevenson; he was to be Idaho Territory's only Democratic governor and also the first territorial governor who was an Idaho resident at the time of his appointment.

Stevenson faced several major issues as governor. He strongly opposed efforts to drive the Chinese out of Idaho by unlawful means, and played a moderating role in the anti-Mormon efforts in southern Idaho. He worked to give territorial governments more authority over their governance and, when those efforts failed, he became an advocate for statehood.

In the meantime, Nevada was rapidly losing population and looked north at the possibility of merging with southern Idaho, while in northern Idaho there was strong sentiment to merge that part of the state with Washington. Stevenson played a leading role in lobbying both Congress and President Cleveland, who had appointed him and was a close friend, to oppose that legislation. In the end, although it passed both the House and Senate, the President subjected it to a pocket veto and the issue was finally dead. Stevenson then moved his efforts to attaining statehood. Even though he left office in 1889, he continued to play a leading role in both establishment of an Idaho Constitutional Convention and in advocating for Idaho's admission as a state.

In 1894, Stevenson ran unsuccessfully for governor. The campaign effort resulted in declining health and he sought out a better climate by moving to the Monterey area in California. In an attempt to combat his health issues, he took laudanum, a potent opium-based narcotic. On July 6, 1895, he died from an overdose of laudanum; he was buried at Boise's Pioneer Cemetery.

18 Robert SMYLIE

October 31, 1914 – July 17, 2004. Attorney. Governor. Boise. Buried: Boise, Pioneer Cemetery.

Robert Smylie almost seemed to define the concept of an activist governor in Idaho – few did so much, and with so much relish.

Far from simply holding the office, he spoke often of operating the "levers of power," almost like an operator handling a large and complex piece of machinery, and for comparably constructive purpose; many of his endeavors were cheered on by the Idahoans who elected him to three terms as governor, (lasting a dozen consecutive years) twice as long as anyone had held the office previously. Those who disapproved would eventually manage, in one of Idaho's great political surprises, to deny him a fourth term.

For all that, he was something of a transitional figure. He changed Idaho and especially its state government, but he also marked the end of an era and was in the state, at least for a couple of generations, the last of his kind: A relatively liberal Republican.

One of the many prominent Idahoans who was a native of Iowa, Smylie came to Idaho to go to school, at The College of Idaho in Caldwell. He would serve on the board there in later years and as acting president, and he often made reference to his association with the college. After serving in World War II in the Coast Guard and taking his law degree at George Washington University Law School, he returned to Idaho in 1947. Through his college connections, he got a job as a deputy to the Idaho attorney general, Robert Ailshie.

What followed was one of the fastest ascents Idaho state politics has ever seen. Before 1947 was out Ailshie, who had been in ill health, died, and Governor C.A. Robins appointed Smylie to replace him. After holding the office in the 1950 election, Smylie won a competitive contest for governor in 1954. At the time, governors were limited to one term, but constitutional changes lifting the restriction were made—allowing Smylie to run again in 1958. He won by fewer than 5,000 votes: He was the only Republican statewide official elected that year amid a Democratic sweep. He won a third time in 1962.

During those years, he made a lot happen and enabled a great deal more.

The Idaho state parks system as Idahoans now know it hardly existed before Smylie (nor was there a parks department), and he personally negotiated some of its key pieces, notably Harriman State Park. He pushed through a comprehensive state civil-service operation. Near the end of his third term he judged the time right to support a sales tax, tried and initially rejected by referenda three decades earlier; for it he deserves significant albeit not total credit. He launched the state's outreach toward tourism and expanded its economic development efforts. Much of what he did was a matter of approach: Close management of state departments, for example, in many cases, as at the state department of highways, shaking loose older ways of doing things. And Smylie was probably the most important figure, both as attorney general and in political races for governor, in slamming shut what had been a widespread gambling industry in the state.

All that activism pleased some and not others.

Smylie was close to moderate and liberal Republicans nationally, especially New York governor Nelson Rockefeller, whom he backed for president in 1964; that combined with his in-state efforts infuriated more conservative Republicans, especially the many Idaho backers of Arizona senator Barry Goldwater. In an effort led by Idaho's Republican National Committeewoman, Gwen Barnett, Smylie was defeated by conservative Don Samuelson, who went on to win a single and troubled term as governor. It was in hindsight a political watershed for Idaho, marking the end of liberals and moderates as a strong force within the Idaho Republican Party, and a conservative ascendancy that has continued to this day. It was reinforced when, six years later, Smylie ran for the U.S. Senate, and finished fourth in a four-way primary behind three more conservative candidates. That marked the end of Smylie's political years—and of a strain of Idaho politics that reached back to William Borah.

How to assess this active, successful, and often highly effective governor who eventually was so thoroughly rejected?

He remade state government as much as any governor had (with the possible exception, which he acknowledged, of C.A. Robins). If his backing of a state sales tax, which gave Idaho a far more stable revenue base than its neighbor states have, was not the only reason that it happened, it was certainly a necessary precondition. And Smylie's presence as a major figure in Idaho – *the* major figure – during a period of profound political realignment changed the state in many ways in the years since, even if many of those ways wouldn't necessarily meet with his approval.

19 Joe ALBERTSON

October 17, 1906 – January 20, 1993. Grocery owner. Boise. Buried: Boise, Morris Hill Cemetery.

Joe Albertson had the dual distinction of founding what was arguably the most successful Idaho-based business – at least, during and shortly after his lifetime – and becoming Idaho's greatest philanthropist.

He was born on October 17, 1906, in Yukon, Oklahoma Territory. When he was three, the family moved to Caldwell, Idaho. He graduated from Caldwell High School in 1925 and attended The College of Idaho for two years as a business major. While attending college, he found work as a grocery clerk at the local Safeway store. He soon became manager of the Safeway in Emmett, and then district manager, overseeing more than a dozen stores.

In 1939, with $5,000 he and his wife, Kathryn, had saved, plus $7,500 he borrowed from Kathryn's aunt, he opened his first Albertson's supermarket at 16th and State streets in Boise. His partners in that effort were Leonard Skaggs, another former Safeway division manager, and Tom Cuthbert, an accountant. With the opening of this store, Albertson became one of the pioneers of modern day supermarkets. The following year he opened two more stores, in Nampa and Caldwell. By the third year of operation, revenues had exceeded $1 million.

Albertson took a great deal of personal interest in the running of his stores. He was a familiar face around the Boise outlets, often standing near the checkout station bagging groceries and greeting customers. Much of the store's marketing focused on the widely recognized face of Joe Albertson. Following World War II, the

Albertsons chain expanded rapidly, becoming one of the nation's leading chains of grocery stores. At its peak, Albertsons would have more than 2,500 stores in 37 states.

The Albertsons stores became the dominant grocery chain in Idaho, and perhaps its most important retail component. Even after the sale of the company in the new century to SuperValu, Albertsons stores continue to dominate the Idaho grocery scene. The combination of employment and spinoff businesses have added to their impact, far different than what Idaho might have seen if another national company had become dominant in the field.

Albertson's philanthropy began with The College of Idaho. In fact from 1991 to 1997 (without the support of Joe Albertson) the name of the college was changed to Albertson College of Idaho.

He and his wife established the J.A. and Kathryn Albertson Foundation in 1966. After Joe Albertson passed away, Kathryn donated $660 million to the foundation. Since then the foundation has donated over $250 million, mostly for education related programs in Idaho. The foundation has become enormously important in shaping, and even effectively setting policy for Idaho public schools and early childhood education. There is no other nonprofit in the state that has compared to the impact it has had in education.

Joe Albertson died on January 20, 1993. Kathryn died on April 30, 2002.

20 Leonard E. "Bill" JOHNSTON

July 4, 1911 - ?. Idaho Falls. Energy site manager. Idaho Falls.

If any single individual deserves credit for "inventing" one of Idaho's largest employers and its largest single government facility, now called the Idaho National Laboratory, it would be Leonard E. "Bill" Johnston. He was the engineer-in-charge who was assigned by the Atomic Energy Commission to develop the National Reactor Testing Station and select a town to house its headquarters.

Johnston was born on July 4, 1911, in South Dakota, and early in his career he showed a knack for heading up large projects. In the 1930s he was executive officer for the U.S. Army Corps of Engineers' Fort Peck District in Montana during the construction of Fort Peck Dam, which made the cover of the first issue of *Life* magazine. During World War II he was involved with the Manhattan Project. In 1946 he was selected to head the Schenectady Operations Office for the AEC. This office headed up a program to conduct nuclear research and development, including the generation of electricity from nuclear power.

The AEC had considered seventy sites across the nation for the National Reactor Testing Station, including Fort Peck and the Arco desert in Idaho. On March 23, 1949, selection of the Idaho location was announced, and Johnston was appointed its manager on April 4. He was visionary, thought strategically, acted diplomatically, and tended to get the job done as quickly as possible. He was the perfect person to invent something that was an entirely new concept to the world: develop a nuclear reactor testing station.

His first move was to select a town for the site's headquarters. Competition was spirited among Pocatello, Arco, Blackfoot, and

Idaho Falls, and there could have been other options. On May 18, only a month after his arrival in Idaho, Johnston announced that Idaho Falls would be the headquarters town. Working out of a local hotel, Johnston next initiated efforts to obtain title to 572,000 acres in the Arco desert. On May 30, construction began on Experimental Breeder Reactor 1. On December 20, 1951, the world's first electricity produced by nuclear fission lighted the town of Arco.

How big a change this was for Arco could be gathered from the *Idaho State Encyclopedia* entry about the town, written not long before: "Points of Interest – There are none of note in the town."

The next several years saw a succession of innovative projects.

In 1952 came the design and construction of the materials test reactor; 1953 was filled with milestones, including the completion of the prototype reactor for the Nautilus nuclear submarine, the construction of the chemical processing plant, and the construction of the first of the boiling water-reactors.

Work began on the U.S. Aircraft Reactor Experiment in 1954. This was an effort to design and construct a nuclear powered bomber. Although the project was eventually canceled, the massive hanger, without a proposed 15,000-foot runway, still exists and the prototype reactors are on public display, along with the EBR 1 reactor.

Johnston served as manager of the NRTS until April 1954. By the time he left it had grown from a staff housed at the Rogers Hotel in Idaho Falls, into a major national laboratory employing thousands of people and providing the economic focus for eastern Idaho.

In the current era, there would have been no equivalent to Bill Johnston. Rather, the decision-making would likely have been replaced by boards, commissions, congressional committees, members of the Idaho congressional delegation, and Washington, D.C.-based bureaucrats.

21 | Frank GOODING

September 16, 1859 – June 24, 1928. Rancher. Governor, Senator. Gooding. Buried: Gooding, Elmwood Cemetery.

Frank Gooding was a governor and a senator – the highest-ranking of the four in this list who held both offices. But remarkably, he is not on this list primarily for what he did in either office. He is here in largest part because of what he founded: the Idaho Republican Party as we know it, and major portions of several key state industries as well.

The industries were, in the main, sheep ranching and banking.

Born in England, Gooding arrived in the United States when he was eight, settling first with his parents at Paw Paw, Michigan. When he turned 18, Gooding and a brother went to California, followed railroad work to Utah and, trying to anticipate another growth area, explored the Wood River Valley, which was in the midst of a mining boom. He had good timing: following the collapse of gold mining in the Wood River Valley in the late 1880s, he bought large tracts of land south of the valley to Shoshone and beyond, on the cheap, and set up big sheep ranches. One of his business partners in this, and later a political ally as well (and his successor in the Senate), was John Thomas, whose sheep operation today is run largely by his grandson, former state senator John Peavey.

Gooding and Thomas (Gooding being the ramrod) were also leaders in bringing Idaho banking into something resembling modern professionalism; it had been mostly a virtual amateur operation up to that point.

From various accounts, he was described as humorless, harsh, and personally disliked by quite a few people who didn't happen to be his allies. Even so, in politics, Gooding left a huge imprint.

In late territorial and early statehood days, the Idaho Republican Party was deeply riven by vicious factional fights, and it still was in 1902, when Gooding became party chair. He was a Main Street business conservative, and one of his opponents was the Progressive William Borah, then becoming steadily more popular. Gooding became the conservative leader when he moved from party chair to governor in 1904 (he was re-elected in 1906), and during that time Borah was elected to the Senate. With his opponent removed from the scene, Gooding organized the state GOP to his liking, and that core organization has sustained the party in Idaho ever since.

Gooding was not inactive as governor or senator, and some of his efforts have resonance. Though a strict fiscal conservative, he pushed through a number of state social services that hadn't existed before, and as senator, while Borah occupied himself with foreign affairs, Gooding pushed through federal reclamation projects in the West.

He also played a big role in Idaho's "trial of the century," involving Big Bill Haywood and others, pressing the case and arranging to bring Haywood and his fellow defendants to Boise to be tried for the assassination of former Governor Frank Steunenberg. He was also a lead negotiator in the setup of national forests in Idaho (though he pushed for smaller reach than materialized).

Gooding was one of the major shapers of Idaho Republican politics and of a collection of industries that have remained important in Idaho ever since.

22 Ray SMELEK

1934 – September 3, 2012. High-tech executive. Boise.

Idaho had largely a natural resource-based economy when Ray Smelek visited for the first time in 1973. His trip that year would do more eventually to diversify Idaho's economy than anyone could then imagine, and would touch off the growth of its high-tech industry.

Smelek was born in Colorado in 1934. His career with Hewlett Packard began in 1957, when as an engineering student at San Jose State University he had an internship with the company. He began working for the company full time after he graduated in 1959. HP was small enough that he was mentored by both Bill Hewlett and David Packard, but it was growing rapidly. Smelek had stints in Palo Alto, England, Scotland, and Mountain View, California. One day he had lunch with Bill Hewlett and some other HP executives, and Hewlett told him that HP was interested in getting into the computer printer business; he wanted Smelek to head up the new division. He also wanted him to determine where the new division would be located.

Hewlett wanted the division to be located someplace other than California, and he gave Smelek the authority to decide where. His selection crew narrowed possible locations down to cities in Arizona, New Mexico, Wyoming, Nevada, Utah, Idaho, Washington, and Oregon. They then narrowed down the list to three cities: Boise, Spokane, and Corvallis. The company's criteria included affordable housing, cultural diversity, low crime, and quality of life.

They visited Boise in February 1973. While Smelek and his four-member committee met with Governor Cecil Andrus, Boise mayor Dick Eardley and various local business leaders, his wife familiarized herself with schools, recreational activities, cultural opportunities, and other family related subjects. Governor Andrus listened to their presentation and immediately said, "Let's do it." Smelek agreed. He later wrote that his family's favorable reaction to Boise was a key factor in the decision.

For the first three months HP's Boise operations were located in the historic Eastman Building. They were the building's last tenants before it burned and was torn down.

The company purchased 100 acres in west Boise. Construction began and by the end of 1975 it had 300 employees in Idaho. At that same time, research and development work began on a new type of printer using laser technology. From this work came, in 1984, the LaserJet printer, which would revolutionize printers for both commercial and home use. In coming years, HP would also locate its Memory Disk and Storage Systems divisions in Boise, with Smelek in charge of them. By 1988, Smelek was heading up, in addition to the Boise operations, HP's activities in Greeley, Colorado and Bristol, England; manufacturing operations in Boise and Grenoble, France; and marketing centers in England, Germany, California, Singapore, and Japan.

In Idaho, HP became for a time the state's largest single private employer. Its presence also attracted many new start-up companies providing goods and services to HP. That marked the beginning of Idaho's high-tech revolution, which would eventually see numerous other companies, including Micron Technology, establishing businesses in Idaho. Technology now makes up about 25 percent of Idaho's gross domestic product.

In March, 1992, Smelek was promoted to become an HP vice president. He retired from HP in 1994, after 37 years with the company. Following his retirement from HP, he led several other Boise high-tech businesses, including Extended Systems and The Network Group. He died shortly before this book's publication.

23 James McCLURE

December 27, 1924 – February 26, 2011. Attorney. U.S. Senator. Payette. Buried: Boise.

One of the great Idaho quandaries:

Some of the people on this list were overturners of old orders, revolutionaries (of an Idaho stripe), or people with little patience for incremental changes. James McClure was not any of these, certainly not as a personality or as evidenced by his resume. And yet he as well as anyone he personifies the overturning of a long-standing Idaho political and policy order, and a move toward larger and deeper conservatism.

McClure became as important and successful a political figure in the state as any, gradually – paying his dues and following the traditional course of a politician. As a young attorney just out of the University of Idaho law school, returning home to Payette, he practiced law with his father. He became first a small-city attorney, then a county prosecutor. In 1960, at the urging of some local party officials, he ran for and won a seat in the state Senate. He moved up into leadership as assistant majority leader. When an opening arose on the Republican ticket for the U.S. House in 1966 because a plane crash killed the presumptive nominee, he won support for it: One modest step after another, over a period of 15 years.

In that 1966 race he beat an incumbent Democrat in what had been, for all but four of the previous 34 years, a Democratic seat. This was not exactly a revolution either. Because of reapportionment, that district had been changed to include Republican Ada County; without it, he would have lost to the

Democrat. But his six years in the House, in which he gradually won ever-stronger support even in traditionally Democratic areas, proved pivotal not only for his own career but for the party balance throughout the state, especially in northern Idaho. The seat stayed in Republican hands until 1990, and has most years since.

From the House, McClure in 1972 – a Republican year – won two strongly contested elections – a Republican primary for the U.S. Senate seat vacated by the retirement of Len B. Jordan which pitted wings of the Republican Party against each other, and subsequently narrowly winning the general election. As a senator, McClure – in contrast to many recent Idaho Republicans in Congress – did not spend much time with grand rhetorical flourishes. It was not his style. He did spend time on grunt work, on the details: the language of bills, the budget line items, the details of what federal activities were taking place back in Idaho. He was a major reason the Idaho National Laboratory got as big as it did, but not because of a single massive effort: More a relentless pounding at it, year after year. He was well-positioned to act: McClure was only Idaho's third senator to chair a full Senate committee (Energy and Natural Resources), and one with direct impact on the state. Few Idaho legislators have left so many subtle marks on Idaho.

So it went politically, sometimes hardly even remarked-on at the time. As a lawyer and as a skilled politician, McClure learned when to negotiate and when to ease his position. He was personally a pleasant person who never lost his comfortable small-town demeanor; people might vote against him on issues, but never against him personally. Without losing his conservative base, he eased the wars with the moderates and began a process of winning over culturally conservative Democrats, a process that led directly to the massive inroads Republicans have made in northern Idaho.

McClure, in his quiet, unassuming and even modest way, was central in the alignment of Idaho politics for decades to come, well into the new century. Considering his own undefeated record of 30 consecutive years in office (from state Senate to U.S. Senate) and his impact on Republican politics in the years since, he is surely the most successful political figure in Idaho in the last half-century.

24 C.W. MOORE

November 30, 1835 - September 20, 1916. Merchant. Boise. Buried: Boise, Morris Hill Cemetery.

Ask many Americans to name things and ideas they identify with the settlement of the American West, and their list will include covered wagons, prospectors, mule trains, and rugged individualism.

C.W. Moore encompassed all that and more. He is on this list for something else, however: He was the real founder of Idaho's banking industry.

Christopher Wilkinson Moore was born in Toronto, Canada, on November 30, 1835. In 1852 he and his family, then in Wisconsin, decided to load their belongings into a wagon and go west to seek their fortune. Arriving in California, Moore spent the next few years on several jobs, including buying and selling livestock. In 1862, the gold bug bit him and he went first to Powder River, Oregon, and then to the gold fields near Elk City, Idaho. As was true with most prospectors of the era, he soon discovered there was little money to be made in that pursuit. But he also determined that there *was* money to be made supplying goods and services to the miners.

Moore went into partnership with Benjamin M. DuRell and purchased a pack string of forty-two mules. They began shipping supplies to the miners and in 1863 turned their focus to the newly discovered prospects of the Owyhee Mountains. Supplies were shipped first from Oregon to Boise by mule and then to Ruby City, DeLamar, and Booneville. Moore and DuRell built a store in Ruby City, the first county seat of Owyhee County, where they provided banking services and sold supplies. In 1865 they opened a store in Silver City.

In 1864, Moore met a visitor to Ruby City from West Virginia. Catherine Minear's brother was operating a stamp mill near Ruby City and she came out to visit him. They were married on July 3, 1865. They built a home in Ruby City and began a family that would eventually include seven children. Idaho would become a state on their twenty-fifth wedding anniversary.

In 1867 the Moores moved to Boise. C.W., joining with DuRell, Governor David Ballard, and others jointly received the second national bank charter west of the Rockies. On March 11, 1867, the First National Bank of Idaho began operations in Boise and Silver City. Five years later Moore bought out DuRell and became the bank's president, a position he would continue to hold until his death in 1916.

The First National Bank would be Idaho's leading bank for more than a century. Moore, more than any other individual, was the father of Idaho banking. He set the pattern for future corporate executives in Idaho being leaders in community improvement ventures and major philanthropy.

Moore was also one of the founders of the Artesian Hot and Cold Water Company, which tapped into a hot spring in east Boise and began providing natural hot water to heat homes and other buildings in Boise. He constructed a mansion on Warm Springs Avenue in Boise that was the first home in the United States to be heated with natural hot water, leading the way to the eventual geothermal heating of much of Boise's business district, as well as the state capitol and the Boise State University campus.

Moore was also heavily involved in community service activities, including the Children's Home, the Methodist Church and the Pioneer Society. That spirit continues today with the Laura Moore Cunningham Foundation, one of Idaho's leading philanthropic organizations.

25 Lafayette CARTEE

1823 – September 2, 1891. Surveyor. Boise. Buried: Pioneer Cemetery, Boise.

As the first surveyor general of Idaho Territory, Lafayette Cartee conducted many of the original land surveys in Idaho. His was a position of major significance in the territory, since most of its interior was unmapped. He surveyed land claims, townships and section lines. In addition he established the initial point near Boise for the intersection of the first parallel and the first meridian, from which all Idaho surveys originate.

Lafayette Cartee was born in 1823 in Tioga County, New York. He had little schooling and was mostly self-educated. But in 1844, he became a school principal in Kentucky and in 1846 he joined the faculty of St. John's College in Cincinnati as a professor of mathematics and civil engineering. He headed west to Oregon Territory in 1850 and established an engineering and surveying business. Cartee was soon elected to the Territorial House of Representatives and in 1854 was elected to the first of two terms as Speaker of the House. His wife died in 1862 and the next year he moved to Idaho with his four children. That same year he constructed the first sawmill at Rocky Bar and also attempted to bring in the first stamp mill into the area. That effort was thwarted by Indian hostilities.

In 1866, Congress established the position of surveyor general for Idaho Territory. Cartee was appointed to the position by President Andrew Johnson and confirmed by the U.S. Senate.

Cartee was also the father of the nursery business in Idaho. He built a commercial greenhouse in 1871 and established Idaho's first large nursery. It was a major undertaking. He imported trees and shrubs from throughout the United States and many foreign countries, bringing them into Idaho by wagon from their rail destination in Utah. He grew enough fruit and vegetables that he produced 30,000 cans a year from his cannery.

Lafayette Cartee passed away on September 2, 1891, the year after Idaho achieved statehood.

Three of Cartee's four children played roles in Idaho's early history. His son Ross married Leona Hailey, the daughter of John Hailey, pioneer stagecoach line operator, territorial delegate to Congress, and founder of the Idaho State Historical Society. His daughter Carrie married Freemont Wood, a U.S. attorney for Idaho and district judge who presided over the Haywood murder trial. His daughter Ella married H.C. Reed a Caldwell attorney and became secretary to John Hailey, the first curator/librarian of the Idaho State Historical Society.

If Lafayette Cartee had not conducted Idaho's initial surveys, someone else would have. But had they not been completed in the timely and accurate way Cartee did them, or made different judgment calls, the territory could have faced severe difficulties. Cartee's surveys made it possible for the federal government to transfer ownership of tracts of land to private individuals, for individuals to file proper mining claims and, following statehood in 1890, for the federal government to turn over land to the state for such purposes as educational endowments. His nursery stock helped to domesticate the state, while the output of his cannery provided preserved food for many of the pioneer settlers of southwestern Idaho.

26 C.A. ROBINS

December 8, 1884 – September 20, 1970. Physician. Governor. St. Maries. Buried: Lewiston, Lewis Clark Memorial Gardens.

Robert Smylie, widely considered one of the most important of Idaho governors (and not known for hiding his own light under a bushel), has said that the most important Idaho governor of all was his predecessor once removed, the man who "set my feet on the rainbow" – but he had plenty of reason to say that aside from the personal connection. More than any other one person, Charles Armington Robins was the governor who pulled Idaho government into the twentieth century.

C.A. Robins was, like so many Idaho governors (including Smylie), born in Iowa. He was raised in Colorado, studied medicine in Chicago, and practiced there as a physician. But after serving in World War I, he sought a small-town life and set up practice in St. Maries; he often was referred to as "Doc" Robins. He became the operator as well of the local hospital and active in the community generally, as county health officer and on the school board. He was elected to the state Senate three times starting in 1938 and made such a favorable impression that in 1943 he was elected president *pro tempore*. After that term he decided to stay put in St. Maries. But that didn't last long.

Robins was such a well-appreciated figure that not only many Republicans but also a lot of Democrats supported him. When time came to nominate candidates for the newly reconfigured four-year term as governor, Republicans seized on Robins to run, and he won easily.

The legislative session that followed, in 1947, turned out to be as important as any in Idaho history, and Robins' involvement was crucial. The biggest issue, and one that progressed only after Robins became heavily involved, was an overhaul of the public school system that included (though was not limited to) compressing the state's 1,118 school districts into a little over a tenth as many.

That alone was a remarkable political and legislative feat, but Robins also rapidly set up the state's first comprehensive building program; much of what is now the Capitol Mall is a result. He created the State Tax Commission, the state's revenue agent, which has operated essentially unchanged since. He helped push through creation – in effect, though the details would take a while to jell – of what is now Idaho State University at Pocatello. He proposed a state department of labor and regulation of oil and gas in the state. He also was able to push through creation of an independent state highway department, diminishing the rawer politics that had governed that area. He pushed through a string of smaller-scale improvements as well, in areas from corrections to worker compensation.

More broadly, but less lasting, he provided leadership and a starting push for an era of progressive Republicanism in Idaho that existed side by side with conservatives, till the latter began to wipe it out in the mid-'60s. Robins' example was the template for the 12-year governorship of Robert Smylie.

Robins never ran for office again after his one term as governor. But that was long enough. He had set a new and different standard for governors, and turned Idaho government, in many ways, into what it is today.

Term-limited in 1950, Robins retired from politics and eventually moved to Lewiston, where he died in 1970. At his funeral service observers noted the church was filled with doctors and nurses, but few politicians. In twenty years he had become almost politically anonymous.

27 Ezra Taft BENSON

August 4, 1899 – May 30, 1994. Farming, agricultural research. Boise. Buried: Whitney, City Cemetery.

Imagine that someone is thought by a third of all Idahoans to be a prophet who is God's spokesman to the entire world. Imagine that same person is the leading official of the federal government agency that has the greatest direct impact on Idaho's largest industry. And that he often speaks out on political ideas that are, to say the very least, controversial.

Meet Ezra Taft Benson.

Benson was one of those rare individuals who were born and grew up in Idaho, had some modest influence in the state while living there, but had the greatest influence on Idaho after moving out.

Born in the small southeastern Idaho town of Whitney (between Preston and Franklin just north of the Utah line) on August 4, 1899, Benson received a bachelor's degree from Brigham Young University and a master's degree from Iowa State University. After receiving his master's, he returned to Whitney to run the family farm, and soon went to work for the University of Idaho as the county extension agent for Franklin County. He moved to Boise in 1930 to accept a statewide position in which he advised farmers on marketing strategies and on establishing farm cooperatives. He also founded the University of Idaho's Department of Agricultural Economics. These alone were substantial accomplishments.

While in Boise he became president of the local LDS stake and oversaw construction of the church's Boise stake tabernacle, making him a key leader in the development of the Mormon community in southwestern Idaho.

In 1939 Benson was named executive director of the National Council of Farmer Cooperatives and moved to Washington, D.C.

Four years later Benson became a member of the LDS Quorum of Twelve Apostles, a position he would hold for the next 42 years. Then, in 1953, President Dwight Eisenhower appointed him Secretary of Agriculture, a position he would hold for the full eight years of Eisenhower's administration. During this time, Benson also became an increasingly outspoken opponent of socialism and communism.

With Idaho's strong LDS population, his politically conservative statements and writings had great sway. He was especially outspoken in his opposition to the civil rights movement and the "new world order," while heaping praise on the John Birch Society. He was undoubtedly a major influence in the rapid growth of the Idaho political right wing in the early sixties, and on the near-win in the state by Republican Barry Goldwater in 1964.

In 1973 he became president of the Quorum of the Twelve Apostles and in 1985, following the death of LDS president Spencer Kimball, became president of the church. The president of the church is viewed as a prophet and is the only man empowered to receive revelation for the entire church and to clarify doctrine. As a result, since an estimated 30 percent of Idaho's population has membership in the church, it may be that that no single individual had more influence in Idaho during his 1985-94 church presidency.

Ezra Taft Benson passed away on May 30, 1994, at the age of 94 and is buried in the Whitney, Idaho, city cemetery.

28 George GRIMES/ Moses SPLAWN

Grimes: ? - August, 1862. Miner. Idaho City. Buried: Pioneerville (open site).

Splawn: December 20, 1835 – August, 1862. Miner. Idaho City. Buried: Yakama, Washington, Tahomah Cemetery.

The reason there is a Boise is that there was a Boise Basin mining area, a massive gold and precious minerals development based around Idaho City that attracted tens of thousands of people at its peak. The two men who found gold there, and started the rush and along with it the impetus to significant white settlement in southwestern Idaho, were George Grimes and Moses Splawn.

They should not be overrated (and indeed, considering the consequences of their find they're not rated especially high). Following the Pierce gold strike of 1860, Idaho was crawling with prospectors hoping to find the next big lode. If not Grimes and Splawn, then someone else would have found the Boise Basin gold. Further, they did just that one thing: To them can't really be attributed the many twists and turns the region's history has taken since.

Still, but for them, some other mining operation might have been the big deal when federal troops came west during the middle and end of the Civil War, looking to build protective forts. It could have been that the first major southern Idaho supply center, in that era just as the territory was beginning to coalesce, developed around Yellow Pine, or in the Wood River Valley. Grimes and Splawn happened to luck into their find at a particular time. And at that moment in Idaho history, timing amounted to a great deal.

Moses Splawn was one of the earliest prospectors to come into the area that would later be named Idaho; he may have entered the territory as early as 1860. He spent time at Orofino, Warren, Elk City, and Florence, at the time the most productive mining areas in Idaho, before becoming co-leader of the party that would discover the largest gold strike in the territory.

Splawn was born on December 20, 1835, in Cravensville, Missouri. In 1852 the family joined a wagon train with fifty wagons and migrated to Oregon's Willamette Valley. In 1853 Splawn left home to prospect for gold, first in southern Oregon and then in British Columbia. In 1860 or '61 he arrived in Idaho. He filed a claim near Pierce in 1861 and then filed subsequent claims elsewhere in north central Idaho. As winter set in, he decided to go to Walla Walla. Camping out one night near modern-day Riggins, he met an Indian named Bannock Louie who told him about a basin to the south that contained heavy deposits of a yellow mineral.

The spring of 1862, Splawn joined a party of fifty prospectors going to search for the legendary Lost Blue Bucket Mine. Arriving in southern Idaho near the Owyhee Mountains, Splawn tried, without success, to get the party to go north in search of the basin. Eventually he did talk six of the members of the party into joining him. At the mouth of the Owyhee River they ran into another party, led by George Grimes, that was going to attempt to connect with the larger party they had just left. Splawn told them that it would be a waste of their time and suggested that they join up with his party in search of the basin. The miners traveled north to what would become Boise and then over the mountains to Clear Creek, then over more mountains to Grimes Creek. They began panning for gold and soon had a collection of nuggets worth $50-$75. The date was August 2, 1862. This was the beginning of the biggest gold rush in Idaho's history.

The area contained numerous Indians hostile to their mining efforts. On August 9, in an altercation with a group of Indians, Grimes was shot in the chest and died.

Although there has been general agreement that Grimes was shot and killed by Indians, rumors have circulated that Grimes was actually killed by members of the prospecting party. He was buried above Pioneerville, on Grimes Pass.

Little is known of Grimes other than he was apparently born in New York, although the date is unknown.

At some point, probably prior to 1860, he migrated to Oregon. He married a woman named Marietta and had a daughter, Rosa. They remained in Oregon when he came to Idaho. However, in July 1864, two years after his death, Marietta traveled to Boise unsuccessfully seeking to take ownership of his mining claims.

Splawn sold his claims before he realized just how valuable they were. Presumably he continued prospecting. Perhaps into the Owyhees. In 1865 he was in Texas visiting family where he got into an altercation with a soldier and shot him. With no trial, the authorities decided to hang him. As he stood on the gallows, he began to incite the spectators gathered to witness the hanging to free him. His exhortations proved successful, the citizens quickly sided with him and, since they outnumbered the authorities, he was set free.

Splawn had a number of other memorable adventures before ending up in central Washington, spending most of his time in the out of doors prospecting, often staying at the homes of family members in the area. He also spent time writing poetry.

On July 7, 1925, at the age of eighty-nine, he was attempting to walk across the street in Yakima and was struck and killed by a passing truck. He was buried in Tahoma Cemetery in Yakima. His was a remarkable life that ran from the age of wagon trains and gold rushes to the motorcar.

29 Harry L. DAY

December 12, 1865 – November 19, 1942. Business developer. Wardner. Buried: Spokane, Holy Cross Cemetery.

If ever there was a poster child for the idea that hard work and persistence leads to success, it could be Harry Day. He had the vision to take a nearly inaccessible section of a hillside and, after many years of hard labor and minimal return, turn it into one of Idaho's great fortunes.

Harry Loren Day was born in Dayton, Nevada, on December 12, 1865. His father, Henry Day, had moved from mining camp to mining camp in California and Nevada seeking his fortune and, in 1887, moved his family to Wardner, Idaho (up the hill from Kellogg), and established a dairy and then a store to supply the miners in the area.

In 1889, while working at his father's store, Harry and Fred Harper decided to seek out a promising mining claim that could hold some promise of development. In a steep hillside, midway between Murray and Wallace, they came across some promising surface ore. Driving a tunnel underground, they and some other partners labored for years to develop the property, which they called the Hercules. Years went by and Harry Day, above all others, remained convinced that at some point they were going to strike it rich. Finally, on June 1, 1901, they did. They struck a vein of ore that assayed out at 133 ounces of silver per ton of ore, a truly astonishing discovery. From 1901-1905, they produced 37,034 tons of crude ore averaging 78.9 ounces of silver per ton. From 1906 until 1925, when the mine closed, it yielded another 709,682 tons of ore concentrate with 36.1 ounces of silver per ton and 47.3 percent lead content.

In addition to discovering the Hercules, Harry Day was also a strong administrator. Keeping the Hercules as primarily a family venture involving his parents and brothers and sisters, plus a few outside partners, he developed a business model that had not been seen before with a mining venture of this type. In addition to the mine, under Harry's leadership, they acquired concentrating mills, smelters, a refinery, a newspaper, a bank, and real estate.

Day family partners included a remarkable, often changing, cast of characters. An early partner, for a brief period, was Harry Orchard, later convicted of murdering Governor Frank Steunenberg. Edward Boyce, a socialist and president of the radical Western Federation of Miners, married Harry Day's sister Eleanor and they became multi-millionaires. Al and May Hutton were strong union supporters; he drove the train that took the miners to blow up the Bunker Hill mill.

Harry Day was also involved in politics and civic affairs, serving as secretary of the Idaho Senate in 1899 and Idaho commissioner to the Pan-Pacific Exposition in 1915. He was also the first president of the modern day Idaho Mining Association and a member of the Idaho Defense Council during World War I.

Although the Hercules was mined out and closed by 1925, the Day interests were reorganized as Day Mines, Inc. Harry retired to his home near Santa Barbara, California and pursued his passion for sailing, target shooting, and collecting western Americana. The new company, headed by Harry's son Henry, would hold 771 mining claims covering over 15,000 acres in Idaho's Shoshone County, second only to Bunker Hill. In 1980 Day Mines was bought out by Hecla Mining.

Day probably was the most important single figure in developing the Silver Valley and turning it into an international mining center, and the central transitional figure between the early wild western mining atmosphere in the valley, and the modern industry that has prevailed there since.

30 Duane HAGADONE

September 3, 1932 - . Business executive. Coeur d'Alene.

Few people can claim to have singularly changed the direction of a community, but Duane Hagadone has done that and much more.

He grew up in Coeur d'Alene where his father was publisher of a small daily newspaper owned by the E.W. Scripps Company. At his father's insistence he attended the University of Idaho but quit during his freshman year and went to work selling newspaper subscriptions in the Silver Valley. He then began selling advertising and was soon earning more money in advertising commissions than his father was earning as publisher.

When his father died unexpectedly in 1958, Hagadone, at age 26, was asked by Scripps to take over as publisher of the Coeur d'Alene paper. Under his direction the paper began to grow until it was one of Scripps' most successful. Scripps asked him to take more responsibility within their chain, which he did in return for a financial interest in the papers they were buying.

Eventually the Hagadone Division of Scripps owned 17 papers. When he and the Scripps brothers divided up their ownership, Hagadone became sole owner of six newspapers. This was the beginning of the Hagadone Corporation.

In the 1980s, Hagadone acquired the North Shore Hotel, in the city on the shore of Lake Coeur d'Alene and expanded it to the luxury facility known as the Coeur d'Alene Resort. The resort includes a marina, spa, and 18-hole golf course made famous for its movable 14th-hole green that floats on the lake.

The Hagadone Corporation expanded to own nineteen newspapers in four states, other publishing interests in two states, several hotels in northern Idaho, and property management of luxury apartments in Coeur d'Alene.

Coeur d'Alene remains the headquarters of the Hagadone Corporation, with offices located on a pier that extends out over the lake next to the Coeur d'Alene Resort. What was, at the time of Hagadone's birth in 1932, a small logging town with a population of 7,000, has become one of the nation's leading resort towns, hosting visitors and conventions from throughout the United States.

Hagadone has become one of Idaho's wealthiest citizens. In a video biography on the organization's web site he said that "I haven't worked a day in my life. I love what I do."

What he has done has transformed Coeur d'Alene from a sleepy timber town to an up-to-date international resort destination. Coeur d'Alene's natural assets may be abundant, but there's no reason to think that transformation would have unfolded as it did but for Hagadone.

31 Moses ALEXANDER

November 13, 1853 – January 4, 1932. Merchant. Governor. Boise. Buried: Boise, Morris Hill Cemetery.

Moses Alexander is known now mostly as the first elected Jewish governor in the United States. That fact in itself had little impact on Idaho.

But Alexander *was* one of the state's most important governors, for three other reasons.

Born in Obrigheim, Bavaria, Alexander came to the United States at 13 and worked for some years at the family retail business at Chillicothe, Missouri. He was elected mayor there, as he would be in Boise. But by 1891 he was headed west, settling in the new town of Boise and promptly launching another retail business, a men's clothing store which grew into a chain, which continue on through a line of succession. He also co-founded the city's first synagogue, Beth Israel.

It may be that a man so accustomed to launching things in private life simply carried over the practice to public office. Alexander was elected mayor of Boise in 1897 and again in 1901. He was a busy mayor, cracking down on gambling, professionalizing the Boise Fire Department and limiting (eliminating would then have been unthinkable) local prostitution.

Prominent by then in Idaho Democratic circles, Alexander made two unsuccessful runs at the governorship before winning it in 1914. He was re-elected two years later, and evidently enjoyed the job enough to seek it once more, in 1922, but unsuccessfully.

So how did he change Idaho?

The least of his impacts, perhaps, was that he was the driving force behind Idaho's 1915 acceptance of statewide prohibition, which lasted about two decades and surely had a big impact on people in the state. Alexander ran on that platform in 1914, thundered in favor of it before the Legislature, and pushed it through. Its limited impact was short-lived, since only a few years later prohibition was imposed nationally. But Idaho's anti-liquor laws remained when national prohibition ended in 1933 and vastly complicated matters resulting in the peculiar state store system still in place.

More important was Alexander's role in driving down and out the influence of the Industrial Workers of the World, a radical labor group that Alexander (and others) suspected of alliance with Germany during World War I. The IWW (the "Wobblies") were the linchpin to radicalism in Idaho labor for most of the state's early history, especially in northern Idaho. It had been opposed in some places head-on and with attacks on labor generally as well, which tended to result in worker sympathy for them. Alexander took a different tack. He attacked the Wobblies as unpatriotic and as well criticized many in management; that gave him credibility with the rank and file, and he succeeded in moderating most of Idaho labor. Idaho labor history took a decisive turn from that period.

Third, as part of the World War I effort, Alexander pushed farmers in southern Idaho to unite their efforts much more directly than they had before, to produce more food for the troops.

This had some profound, long-range effects. The most concrete was a linking together of the canal and irrigation systems in southern Idaho, which had been much more fragmented previously. That had a tremendous effect on Idaho agriculture, allowing for significant expansion of croplands in southern Idaho. That stronger water system helped sustain Idaho agriculture through the tough economic years of the '20s.

32 Francois PAYETTE

1793 - ? (after 1844). Fur trader. Parma area.

In the 1830s, when control of the Northwest was still very much in the balance between Britain and the United States, Britain periodically held an advantage. From its regional base around Oregon City, the Hudson's Bay Company reached out east to take over the site of a twice-failed fort and supply stop – at the confluence of the Boise and the Snake rivers, near what is now Parma, Idaho – that had failed twice before as a fort and supply stop. A HBC contractor named Thomas McKay set it up in 1834, funded specifically by the company as a company operation – put in place for the benefit of the company and British operators, not for the competing Americans.

That was significant, because there were no comparable American outposts anywhere in the vast surrounding region at a time when many American settlers (notably Oregon Trail settlers), merchants, missionaries, and many others were headed in that direction. The advantage to the British and Canadians of the HBC presence might have been incalculable in this decade before the border issues were finally settled – had they pressed that advantage as hard as they seemed to have intended.

That they did not seems due more than anyone else to Francois Payette (namesake of an Idaho river, a county, and city).

He was a Canadian who came to Fort Boise in 1835 to help McKay, and over the next decade or so took over for him. During that critical period, as the number of Americans traveling through the area swelled, Payette generously opened his doors to all. He was commonly described as a fine host and a humanitarian, ready to help any traveler in the area. (The American mountain man William Craig, noted elsewhere on this list, was only one of his many American guests.)

What his masters at Hudson's Bay thought of this isn't clear, but Payette's increasingly famous assistance seems never to have faltered. And when he left in 1844, his successor, James Craigie, maintained the same approach, though by then the international border issues had largely been settled. The fort lasted into the 1850s, when human conflicts and natural disasters – storms, a rising river and more – finally led to its abandonment.

Conflicting stories, and no historical certainty at all, attach to Payette after his departure from Fort Boise in 1844. We don't know for sure what happened to him after he left Idaho.

What might have happened to early Idaho settlement, and to the Oregon Trail, if Fort Boise had been an obstacle along the way rather than an assist? What if Francois Payette simply had been a very different sort of host?

33 LAWYER (HALLHALHOTSOOT)

? - January 3, 1876. Tribal leader. North-Central Idaho.

The famous friendship that the Nez Perce long had with the early white explorers and settlers did not happen by accident. There was probably no greater Nez Perce proponent for those peaceful relations than Hallhalhotsoot, or Lawyer, as he was known by the whites.

Lawyer was the son of Twisted Hair, a Nez Perce chief, and his mother was a Flathead. He was one of a group of three Nez Perce boys who were the first to see William Clark and his party when they arrived on the Weippe Prairie on September 20, 1805. Twisted Hair helped the expedition members by providing them with shelter, food, and counsel. These were the first whites that any of the Nez Perce, including Lawyer, had ever seen, and they left a lasting impression on him. Lawyer developed a great respect for the whites and even became a dedicated Christian convert.

The name "Lawyer" was bestowed on him by white trappers, perhaps at the Pierre's Hole rendezvous of 1832, which he attended. The trappers admired his ability to debate and his overall shrewdness. He was recognized as a person of great eloquence. Washington territorial governor Isaac Stevens referred to him as an "American Solon," and another as "a consummate diplomat." Lawyer became the chief of his band of Nez Perce. At the 1855 Walla Walla Treaty Council, he represented his band and was actively involved in negotiations.

Although the Nez Perce had numerous bands and numerous chiefs, they didn't have a single "head chief." It was probably Isaac

Stevens who decided to designate Lawyer as the principal chief of the Nez Perce, primarily to enable the whites to rely on a single Nez Perce to sign treaties. As it turned out the Nez Perce Treaty was signed by chiefs of each of the Nez Perce bands; Lawyer signed with the designation of head chief. It established a large reservation that ran roughly from modern Colfax, Washington, to Elgin, Oregon, and east from the Wallowas to modern Challis, Idaho. It also promised schools, lumber and flour mills, a church, blacksmith shop, $100,000 and numerous other items, most of which were never delivered. And, with the discovery of gold on the reservation in 1860, the government not only chose to ignore the treaty boundaries but send in troops to protect the white trespassers.

Many Nez Perce were open in their derision of Lawyer's role in negotiating with the whites, maintaining that he had essentially sold them out. But Lawyer did his best to protect Nez Perce interests. It is likely that Lawyer's efforts kept the two interests at peace far longer than might otherwise have been possible, but it also made him a controversial figure among some tribal members.

Lawyer signed a second treaty in 1863, without the consent of other Nez Perces, that reduced the size of the reservation by roughly 90 percent, but assumed the government would eventually make good on its promises. This again kept the soldiers at arm's length and prolonged peace between the two parties. However, by 1864, even Lawyer had given up on the government fulfilling its promises. In a speech that was both eloquent and bitter delivered in Lewiston in 1864, he talked about all that the Nez Perce had done for the whites and the little the whites had done in return for the Nez Perce. In 1868 he even traveled to Washington, D.C. to demand that the government honor its treaty commitments. In 1870, he voluntarily stepped down from his role as a Nez Perce leader. He died on January 3, 1876, before the beginning of the Nez Perce war of 1877. The bands he influenced did not participate in the war.

Even if some of Lawyer's efforts were controversial among some Nez Perce bands, it would be difficult to overstate the benefits received by white settlers. Regardless, without his mediating influence, the early history of the Inland Northwest would have unfolded much differently.

34 Pinckney LUGENBEEL

November 20, 1819 – March 18, 1886. Military. Boise. Buried: Detroit, Michigan, Elmwood Cemetery.

How's this for an obscure name?

He wasn't even in Idaho for long – he was mostly a Michigander who spent more time in Washington, the Dakotas, and elsewhere than he did in Idaho. He was here when few people were, and that was long over a century ago, and then he left soon after.

Those who walk for the old Fort Boise Army Reserve Center in north Boise may be aware of Lugenbeel Hall at 410 West Fort Street. But they may know little of the man for whom it was named.

He did only one thing of any significance in the history of Idaho.

But that one thing was significant: He made Boise possible.

Pinckney Lugenbeel's short stay in Idaho came in the summer of 1863. Since the previous fall, a massive gold rush had boomed in the Boise Basin mountains to the northeast, and federal officials were concerned about its security, from thieves and from Native Americans.

The right thing, they thought, was to set up a military outpost to protect the gold rush area. That is what Lugenbeel was assigned to do, and did. He was told to pick a site east of the old Fort Boise (near what is now Parma, but which had been abandoned for nine years), but clearly he had latitude in his choice.

The pick was fortuitous. He built a small fort at what is still an Army Reserve park near the main federal building near downtown

Boise. It served its military purpose well, but its location near the Boise River and the foothills also lent more than usual security to civilians who were thinking about settling in the area.

Within days after the major started work on the fort, a group of businessmen mapped a townsite between the fort and the river that is still the center of town. Lugenbeel had essentially set the coordinates of present-day Boise. He also gave strong security to the agricultural and other supply businesses that grew up initially to feed the mining district.

Lugenbeel's choices were probably lucky shots to some degree. But from his decisions we can trace a straight line to Boise's position as Idaho's capital (partly, again, because of its security and decent climate), economic hub, and largest city. He merits a substantial spot on this list.

35 | Charles C. RICH

August 21, 1809 – November 17, 1883. Settlement leader. Buried: Paris, City Cemetery.

There are two main reasons Thomas Ricks ranks close to the top on this list and Charles Rich, who did many of the same sorts of things, ranks lower.

One is that Ricks founded what eventually became the largest private higher education institution in Idaho (Ricks College, later Brigham Young University-Idaho), while Rich left behind no comparably large institution.

Another is that that Ricks's settlement, many miles away from the support of his brethren in Utah, was by no means an inevitable success, but was instead highly risky and a considerable gamble; it might not have evolved in remotely the way did. Rich's settlement, on the Utah border and moving north beyond it, was a more incremental outgrowth of the Utah settlements already in existence. And Rich was that settlement's leader for only a short period of time; William Budge would go on to shape its direction more profoundly.

Even so, his achievements were considerable. Rich, a native of Kentucky, was an LDS missionary even back in the Illinois days, before the church came west, and once in the West he was a leader in the Utah settlement. From there he went to California and to Europe to found mission efforts, and from February 1849 served as a member of the Quorum of the Twelve Apostles. He has a major role in LDS church history overall.

In 1863 Rich was told by Brigham Young to venture north into Idaho to found settlements there. He did that, checking in on (and helping) the fledgling settlement at Franklin, then going on to settle the Bear River Valley, with a central point at what is now Paris. He also founded the first LDS stake in Idaho, setting up the origins of the church's structure north of Utah.

His settlement in the Bear River Valley, more than the smaller one at Franklin, helped provide a base for ongoing LDS agricultural settlements further north in Eastern Idaho. And they have remained in place, continuously and growing and in many places very much along the lines of their origins, in the century and more since they were founded.

36 | Gwen BARNETT

1926 – February 2000. Political Activist.

For most political party activists, impact is measured on an election-by-election basis. Gwen Barnett's impact can be measured over a course of five decades – and running – although the work that resulted in that impact lasted less than ten years.

In the 1960s, Gwen Barnett became the most powerful woman in Idaho and then, nearly overnight, metaphorically fell off the edge of the earth and was never heard from again.

Gwen Hughes was born in Dallas, Texas, in 1926 and was raised in Tulsa, Oklahoma. Following her graduation from high school she attended Stanford University, married Steele Barnett and moved to Idaho, where her husband was an executive with Boise Cascade. In 1963 she was elected Republican National Committeewoman for Idaho. At the time, she was the youngest member of the national committee.

Governor Robert Smylie, who encountered her about then, called her "the philosophical ideologue, field marshal and guru" of the ultraconservative wing of the Idaho Republicans. His description was spot-on, and he would find out just how effective she really was when she played a key role in unseating him in the 1966 GOP primary.

Smylie had by then risen to national prominence. He was strongly allied with the moderate wing of the Republican party, which included Nelson Rockefeller and George Romney. When Barry Goldwater lost the 1964 presidential election, Smylie, as chairman of the Republican Governors' Association, was the first prominent Republican publicly to call for the resignation of Dean Burch as national chairman of the Republican party. Burch was a former Goldwater Senate staffer who had been GOP chair for 1964-65; he was strongly supported by Gwen Barnett, and when he was removed she never forgave Smylie for his role.

Nor did she appreciate Smylie's support of Rockefeller over Goldwater; many of the most active Idaho Republican party people were Goldwater backers.

Smylie's defeat in 1966 has been attributed to many different factors. Gwen Barnett, more than any other single factor, brought it about. She did more: She established the framework for the very conservative side of the Idaho Republican Party, a framework picked up and expanded and employed for decades to come.

Another casualty in Barnett's rise in power was Harley Markham of Pocatello, a member of the Executive Committee of the Republican National Committee. Markham was a close ally of Smylie's and, as a result, drew the wrath of Barnett. In 1964, she engineered an effort, possibly through her friend Senator John Tower of Texas, to have Markham removed from the Executive Committee and replaced by a Texan.

Following Samuelson's defeat by Democrat Cecil Andrus in 1970, she resigned her party office in 1971, as did State Republican Chairman Roland Wilbur of Lewiston. After she divorced Steele Barnett, she and Wilber married and moved to Oregon. After that she disappeared from the Idaho political scene (and never surfaced prominently in Oregon's). But in less than a decade, she had almost single-handedly permanently changed the course of Republican politics in Idaho.

Gwen Barnett Wilber died in Escondido, California, in February of 2000.

37 William CRAIG

c. 1807 – October 16, 1869. Trapper, merchant. Lapwai. Buried: Family land, near Lapwai.

Think of William Craig as the lubricant in a human machinery that might have otherwise broken down. Badly.

Apparently a fugitive from justice in his native Virginia (the nature of his original crim, and possibly his birth name as well, remains unclear), Craig became a mountain man – one of the renowned generation of trappers and hunters around the 1830s. In 1840 he settled near Lapwai, becoming Idaho's first homesteader (apparently, and un-patented) and, crucially, marrying into the Nez Perce tribe.

From that base, and while farming and running sundry small businesses over the years, Craig would serve as the go-between – interpreter, agent, sometimes advocate – for both the Nez Perce and the American governmental, military, and business people circling ever closer. He was trusted much more by both sides than was anyone else in the area, and he frequently managed to avert conflict. Initially more inclined toward the United States point of view, he became increasingly skeptical of his country's methods and expansionist motives.

This positioning made a big difference when time came to determine terms for the Nez Perce reservations (which changed over the years), and especially when Elias Davidson Pierce organized Idaho's first gold rush about 70 miles from Craig's farm, in the Orofino country. Pierce stayed often at the Craig farm and got considerable help from Craig, who hoped that both he and the Nez Perce would benefit financially from the influx of miners. But for

Craig, the Orofino gold rush easily could have led to war. In a larger sense, without his presence and efforts, the Inland Northwest might have developed in dramatically different ways.

It's probably not a coincidence that when the Nez Perce war finally came, in the 1870s, it happened several years after Craig's death.

In north central Idaho, a mountain is named for Craig, as is the city of Craigmont, and there's a Highway 95 roadside historical marker about him. And, unlike some of Idaho's earliest pioneers, he still has family residing in the Pacific Northwest.

38 | James M. GUFFEY

January 19, 1839 – March 20, 1930. Developer. Silver City.

Few would suspect a common thread linking the most successful mining venture of Idaho's Owyhee mines, Swan Falls Dam, the development of the Spindletop oil fields in Texas, Gulf Oil Company, Idaho Power Company and the Mellon family of Pittsburgh. But there was , and his name was James M. Guffey.

Guffey was born in Pennsylvania on January 19, 1839. In his early thirties, he became involved in the development of Pennsylvania's petroleum industry. He then branched out into coal. He had a huge capacity for hard work and quickly became one of the most successful businessmen in Pennsylvania. He also became a close business associate of the Mellon family. In 1891, in partnership with Andrew Mellon, he came to Idaho. He immediately set about buying and merging a number of the most productive mining properties in the Owyhees into the Trade Dollar Consolidated Mining Company. Guffey was president of the company and Mellon was vice president.

It was a turning point in developing of the mining industry in the Owyhees, and contributed heavily to the development of Boise area. The company developed some of the richest silver deposits ever discovered in the United States. As late as 1897, the Trade Dollar was generating net annual profits of nearly $500,000 a year. (Its employees included William D. "Big Bill" Haywood, who later would be charged with, and found innocent of, conspiracy to murder of former Idaho governor Frank Steunenberg.) The company's legal team consisted of Richard Z. Johnson, William E. Borah, and John F. Nugent. Johnson had been Idaho's territorial attorney general,

Borah and Nugent would both go on to serve in the United States Senate, and Nugent became chair of the Federal Trade Commission.

In 1896, Guffey talked Mellon into joining him in financing W.H. Dewey's project to bring the railroad to Owyhee County to serve the Owyhee mines. They constructed a steel railroad bridge across the Snake River and formed the Boise, Nampa and Owyhee Railroad. A small town named Guffey grew up near the site of the bridge. The railroad terminated in Murphy, and from there horse-drawn wagons continued up into the mountains to Silver City nearly twenty-five miles away. The line operated for fifty-one years until it closed in 1947. Although the rails were removed years ago, the Guffey Railroad Bridge still spans the Snake River, while the old town of Guffey is little more than a memory.

As the Trade Dollar continued to prosper, the era of electricity emerged. Up until 1900 the Trade Dollar had depended upon wood to generate its operating power. By then the Owyhees were largely stripped of timber and a new source of power was needed. Under Guffey's direction, the company constructed a hydroelectric generating dam at Swan Falls on the Snake River, with power lines strung to the Trade Dollar. The dam was built at a cost of $250,000. Swan Falls would turn out to be one of the most important dams in Idaho, for water right and other legal reasons, forming one of the cornerstones of Idaho Power Company and Idaho's electric industry.

By 1910, the mining activity was coming to a close in Silver City and the Trade Dollar Consolidated Mining Company formed the Swan Falls Power Company. After a couple of reorganizations, the Swan Falls installation was included in a consolidation of companies that became Idaho Power Company in 1916.

By then, Guffey had moved on to Texas where he financed the development of the first successful well in the legendary Spindletop oil field. He then took out leases on over a million acres of land for drilling, constructed an oil pipeline and built a refinery, all of which would eventually become the Gulf Oil Corporation. In Pennsylvania, Guffey became the leader of the state's Democratic party for a number of years. He died in Pittsburgh on March 20, 1930.

39 | Eugene CHAFFEE

March 10, 1905 – February 5, 1992. College president. Boise.

Boise in the early '30s was Idaho's capital and by far its largest city, but it lacked something several other Idaho cities already had: A college, even a small one. In 1932, the Episcopal Diocese of Idaho offered to work with the Boise Chamber of Commerce to turn the buildings near downtown Boise that housed St. Margaret's Hall, a school for girls, into a small college for women. Boise Junior College expanded gradually in the next few years, but the hard times of the depression led the church to withdraw funding after a couple of years. The barely-there college became the project of a Chamber of Commerce committee.

Scrambling, the committee set up a governing structure that split responsibility among several people and tried to recruit as academic dean the school's social-science teacher, Eugene Chaffee, whose sole administrative background had been a brief run as a public school principal. He turned them down, saying the authority to run the school should be concentrated rather than dispersed, and followed that by saying he was resigning to go to Brazil, to work on his doctoral dissertation in history on that country's boundary disputes. Something must have shook up the governing board at that point. They sat down with Chaffee again and agreed to give him sole executive authority over the institution if he would stay and become its president.

Chaffee did, in June 1936. By the time he retired from that same job, in 1967, the little college had been transformed into a large metropolitan institution on the verge of university status.

Many community leaders in Boise (including several in this list, such as Harry Morrison and Lynn Driscoll) played active roles in promoting the school, but none was so central or pivotal as Chaffee. In his book *Boise College – an Idea Grows* (half history and half memoir), Chaffee describes in detail the complex legislative maneuvering that shifted the institution from private to public status in 1939; Chaffee was the key ingredient in getting that done. He was the leader in finding and obtaining, and developing, the central-Boise site where Boise State University now is based. He pushed the college through to four-year status in 1965 and developed, as his parting gift, a long-term plan for growing the institution in the '70s and beyond – a plan that has been, in many ways, fulfilled.

Idaho's lead institution of higher learning, the University of Idaho, had many parents. Many people affected its growth, but no one person so profoundly influenced its development as to merit a place on this list specifically because of it.

Boise State University, by some measures the state's largest institution now, is another story. Its development and position in the state can fairly be attributed in great part to one person: Eugene Chaffee.

40 James H. HAWLEY

January 17, 1847 – August 3, 1929. Attorney. Governor. Boise. Buried: Boise, Morris Hill Cemetery.

James Hawley, born in Iowa and brought by gold-hunting relatives to California in 1861, ran off a year later – at the age of 15 – after hearing rumors of fantastic gold strikes in the Boise Basin in what had yet to be called Idaho. When Hawley died in Boise in 1929, he was eulogized as one of the last Idaho pioneers, which he was. But more specifically, he pioneered the practice of Idaho law.

He was, to begin with, self-taught, there being no colleges of law (or of any other kind) in the years after he had arrived in the Idaho City area and then concluded that mining wasn't going to make him much of a living. He studied law, briefly "read for the law" with a San Francisco firm, then set up practice.

His legal education may seem thin by today's standards, but his on-the-job training seems to have made up for it: He developed an immense practice.

There were, after all, few lawyers in Idaho at the time. Even bearing that in mind, Hawley's reach and one-on-one impact was tremendous. He was a key figure in the two most prominent court cases in Idaho during his lifetime – the Diamondfield Jack case, in which he argued for the defense, and the Haywood trial, for the prosecution – but more important was the sheer number of cases he handled. By one estimate, he was an attorney of record in a tenth of all of the legal matters filed in Idaho in the 1880s. And his practice ran from the 1860s until well into the twentieth century. He was involved in most of the major Idaho cases of the era, from the

Diamondfield Jack murder case to the appeal which upheld the Idaho Women's Suffrage Act.

Important too was his effectiveness, which shaped much of Idaho law – and politics. William Borah, an attorney (and U.S. Senator) who sometimes battled and sometimes allied with him, was quoted as saying, "Jim Hawley has defended more men, and got them acquitted, and prosecuted more men and got them convicted, than any lawyer in America."

Hawley had specific areas of impact and influence, partly in politics. He served as a Democrat in the territorial legislature, and was a significant figure in Democratic politics from then into early statehood. He won a term as governor in 1910.

But his influence as an attorney probably was his major impact. And it left a specific legacy. At his death he was in legal partnership with his son, Jess Hawley, and the Boise-based law firm Jess Hawley led for many years lasted, grew, and expanded. Known today as Hawley Troxell Ennis & Hawley, it has been for many years the largest business law firm based in Idaho.

41 William DEWEY

August 1, 1823 – May 9, 1903. Businessman. Nampa.

In 1863, immigrants coming to Idaho were arriving by wagon and horseback. Some, coming into Lewiston, even arrived by boat. It was highly unusual for anyone to walk to Idaho, but that is exactly how William H. Dewey arrived. He walked 400 miles from Virginia City, Nevada, to the mountains of Owyhee County, with $27 in his pocket. The trip took eight weeks, and he is rumored to have arrived with no shoes on his feet.

This hard traveler was no youngster. When he arrived on foot in Idaho, he was about 40 years old.

Dewey was born on August 1, 1823, in Adams, Massachusetts. When he was three, the family moved to upstate New York, 52-miles from Buffalo. He left home at 11 after receiving a beating from his mother and walked to Buffalo without shoes, underclothing or a coat. Within four years he owned and operated two barges on the Erie Canal. About 1860, he traveled to San Francisco, where he went into business with Michael Jordan, who would later lead the first team of prospectors into the Owyhee Mountains.

Dewey and Jordan then decided to move to Virginia City, Nevada, and invest all of their money in local mining ventures. They lost everything. In 1862 Jordan left to go to Idaho and seek his fortune. Dewey followed the next year. Within seven years Dewey had become wealthy and Jordan had been killed by Indians.

Dewey was the archetype of a promoter, builder, and organizer. He also could be both flamboyant and reckless. He made a fortune investing in mining properties in the South Mountain area of

Owyhee County and then lost it. In 1886, he purchased and developed the Trade Dollar Mine, which he then sold to Edward Guffey and Andrew Mellon for $1 million.

In true Old West style, he was also involved in one fatal shoot-out incident. Following an argument in a Silver City bar in 1884, he followed the bartender, Henry Koenig, down an alley where they had a shootout. When the smoke cleared, Koenig was dead. Dewey spent six months in the territorial prison in Boise before his conviction was overturned.

He was also involved in road building and community building, establishing the town of Dewey, with a spacious and modern hotel, in 1896. About this same time, a group of investors hoped to greatly expand the ten-year-old town site of Nampa. When they went into default, Dewey bailed them out and, in the process, gained title to over 2,000 Nampa building lots, making him the largest land owner in Nampa. That same year he also took a leading role in establishing the Boise, Nampa and Owyhee Railroad. The line eventually connected Nampa with Murphy, and Emmett.

In 1900, Dewey began one of his most ambitious projects, the construction of an opulent new hotel in Nampa, to be called the Dewey Palace. The three-story brick hotel would cost nearly $250,000 and contained, among other things, a bowling alley, barber shop, ballroom, restaurant, bar, and candy store, as well as many rooms and suites. It even had its own electrical generating plant. When it opened in 1902, it was the finest hotel in Idaho.

Dewey was the real founder of Nampa, today Idaho's second largest city, and his purchases and developments positioned it well for the path of growth, centered on agriculture and industry and close ties to Boise, it has taken since.

Unfortunately, Dewey would only be able to enjoy it for a few months. On May 9, 1903, he died. The Payette newspaper said in reporting his death that he was "probably the most widely known capitalist and promoter of Idaho."

42 Tom BOISE

February 1, 1885 – October 9, 1966. Businessman. Lewiston. Buried: Lewiston, Normal Hill Cemetery.

Think of him as a Democratic counterpart to Lloyd Adams.

When one of the authors compiled in 1990 a list of 13 Idahoans influential in the state's politics, Boise was ranked second. He runs a little lower on this list for several reasons, even apart from its concerns being broader than the purely political. The Democratic Party has diminished in influence since then. Tom Boise's hold and influence on it were essentially wiped out in 1966, only months before he died. And the remnants of the old Democratic loyalties he built were gone by a quarter-century after that, while reverberations of Adams' influence on the GOP continue. Also, Boise was strongly influential over a shorter time, about half as long as Adams.

Having said that, Boise was a substantial figure in Idaho history, far outstripping his (almost non-existent) public profile. His impact on Idaho politics and policy was tremendous for a span of more than 30 years.

The similarities to Adams are in some ways striking. He too was a businessman at a relatively far end of Idaho: Lewiston, in his case. He was a native of that city, growing up next to a then-lively Chinatown, on part of the property where the Lewiston *Tribune* operations are now based. He launched himself into business as a real estate agent, eventually buying and selling substantial properties in town, including Lewiston's Raymond Hotel. Boise played an important role in keeping Lewiston an important regional center during its low period around the twentieth century's turn. He was for many years a Republican (until his conversion during the early New

Deal era) and worked comfortably with Republicans. Ideologically he remained generally conservative, as was the segment of the Democratic party he led.

Following the Democratic dark days of the 1920s, the New Deal era brought that party to the fore. Boise was not part of that, but he was a central player in the Democratic transformation. In the early '30s, the party was dominated by liberal and charismatic figures such as C. Ben Ross, James Pope, and later, Glen Taylor. Boise is a key reason those figures never took over the party. He probably engineered the primary defeat of Pope by the more conservative D. Worth Clark in 1938 and generally moved the party in a more conservative (as he figured, centrist) direction.

He gave that effort bite through his meticulous organization of the party. He interwove it with the burgeoning labor movement, which would reach peak influence and percentage membership in Idaho in the fifties. He organized the detailed precinct organization work the Democratic Party in Idaho has not seen fit to undertake before or since. His organizing capability kept the Democrats from being utterly swamped and destroyed in the low times (such as the elections of 1946 and 1950), and allowed for regular rebounds. His organizational skills also blocked the wide spread of liberal ideology around the state.

All this gave Boise impact in campaign organization and in legislative lobbying. In the latter area, he was a sometime partner, sometime sparring partner, with Republican Adams. A significant number of their achievements can be properly given dual credit.

Boise's impact came to an abrupt and smashing halt in 1966, months before he died.

The occasion was the first gubernatorial race of Democrat Cecil Andrus, which he lost to a Tom Boise-backed candidate – who only weeks after the primary died in a plane crash. At the party meeting called to replace that candidate, Andrus went head to head against the Boise faction, who now backed former Senator Max Hanson. Boise, at that time, was ill and confined to a hospital bed in Spokane. It was a moment of crisis for the party, at which Senator Frank

Church and other leading Democrats weighed in for Andrus, and by a narrow vote broke Boise's influence over the party machinery.

That event, remembered with clarity for decades by people who participated in it, was a turning point for Idaho's Democratic party.

In one sense, this matters historically only little, in that Boise had only months to live. In another sense, however, Church and Andrus in effect broke the Democratic Party organization that Tom Boise had largely built (and which never recovered) by replacing it with their own. When Church and then Andrus left Idaho elective politics, the party had no strong organization to fall back on.

43 Harry MORRISON

February 23, 1885 – July 19, 1971. Construction contractor. Boise. Buried: Boise, Morris Hill Cemetery.

There's a lot you can say about Harry Morrison and the company he co-founded, the Morrison-Knudsen Company, that does not speak directly to his influence in Idaho.

M-K was a big building company, and Morrison was a major figure in the industry – he appeared on the cover of the May 3, 1954 *Time* magazine as a builder "to tame rivers and move mountains," the incarnation of an article about "Builders Abroad." M-K built the Hoover Dam, military facilities in World War II, infrastructure for the National Aeronautic and Space Administration space shots of the '60s, and massive structures all over the globe.

Based at Boise throughout its history (until the company's 1996 bankruptcy and subsequent takeover by Washington Construction, in its current iteration called URS), it was a very big deal in global construction, one of the largest in the field. One stat: The company built more than 150 dams, many of them among the largest in the world.

A little closer to home, you could say that Morrison (and his partner, Hans Knudsen) were the link between the federal water reclamation projects of the early 1900s and the development of Boise as a city known for its corporate headquarters. Morrison and Knudsen started as labor help on some of the early reclamation projects, then saw an opportunity to make money by subcontracting some of the work themselves, starting with a pumping station at Grand View (their first project). The company grew steadily and rapidly, starting with midsized Idaho projects and moving on to larger efforts, further afield.

But Harry Morrison's influence on Idaho extended beyond dam-building.

He and his family were involved in many civic matters; Morrison was an important figure behind developing what is now Boise State University.

More critical is his business activity. For example, during the Depression he spent countless days and months working to keep the Idaho First National Bank solvent and operating.

His decision to keep M-K headquarters in Boise made it the first large corporate headquarters, predating Albertsons and J.R. Simplot by decades, and proved that a major international corporation could be run successfully from the city.

From its first one-room downtown office in 1912, M-K grew into a major corporate concern by the time of mass construction in the New Deal '30s, at a point when Boise's population had yet to see 40,000 and when transportation links to the larger world were far more primitive than they would be a generation later. The ability of this world-wide corporation to put down roots in Boise *and* do global business from there, must have been a great encouragement to people like Joe Albertson and J.R. Simplot as they too decided to keep their businesses home. And the collection of business magnates that developed in the '40s, '50s and '60s changed Boise's, and Idaho's, social and political environment in important ways, making this still-small city much more independent in tone than many other, larger communities.

44 Drew STANDROD

? - 1943. Attorney. Pocatello.

Many Pocatellans probably have taken notice, or at least heard, of the Standrod Mansion on North Garfield, one of the most notable large residences dating from around statehood.

Few probably have an idea that, or why, at several critical points around statehood, its builder Drew Standrod was one of the most pivotal figures in Idaho.

After heading west in the mid-1870s from Kentucky, he set up law practice in Malad and became district attorney, best known at the time for his prosecution of Mormons. That gave him the local and regional political leverage for serving in the Idaho constitutional convention.

One of the first district judges in eastern Idaho, and a member of the governing board of a number of regional banks (including the D.L. Evans and Ireland banks), he also was one of the most influential figures in developing both the legal and banking professions in eastern Idaho. (He was also one of the founders of the still-standing Yellowstone Hotel in Pocatello.)

More significant for the state, he was one of the first three members of the new Public Utilities Commission in 1913 and evidently was the leading figure there in establishing just how the state would go about regulating such fast-growing utilities as electric power and telephone.

Those limits were not foregone conclusions, and Idaho was very much, even in those days of progressive politics, a small-government state.

Standrod's most pivotal actions, though, came at the constitutional convention. In his book on the convention, *The Ties that Bind*, writer Dennis Colson called Standrod "the father of Idaho water law." His role in the sometimes hot debate evidently was subtle, but the results were large-scale: The rules for use of water in Idaho fundamentally have shaped the state, from then to now.

45 Frank F. JOHNSON

Banker, utility executive. Boise.

Few private organizations have been so important in Idaho, over so long a period, as Idaho Power Company. Not only has it supplied electricity for much of the state's population for most of the state's history, but its developments (especially in hydropower) and the resulting generally low power rates have greatly influenced agricultural and other development nearly since statehood. It has been an important player in developing Idaho.

In that corporate history, Frank F. Johnson stands out, because his efforts made possible what followed.

Things could have gone in other directions, because Idaho's electric power situation at the opening of the 20th century was less organization than it was chaos.

In its early stages, power suppliers were local, small, and primitive. In 1887, Hailey and then Boise could claim to have electric power, but in small amounts and in limited areas; only small turbines were needed to supply the small amounts of power involved. The business bar to entry was very low, and across southern Idaho about 50 individual electric power companies sprang up. Some (such as a couple of generators at Pocatello) were moderate in size, but most were tiny, and there was little, if any, inter-organizational cooperation.

The demand for power was growing rapidly, however, and soon the many companies were consolidated through buy-outs. In 1906 there were just 19 companies left in the area from Boise to Pocatello, but the field was turbulent with the fast growth of farming reclamation land in the Magic Valley, and work on hydropower dams in the Snake River (mainly the Swan Falls Dam). The companies kept swallowing each other, reducing the numbers even more, but the chaos took its toll. By 1915, the five companies remaining were all in financial trouble, and three were in "receivership" – virtually bankrupt.

Then in 1916, they merged, and the combine of the five became Idaho Power Company.

It might have failed but for Johnson.

Johnson, a native of Wisconsin, had some background as an engineer (and as a rancher and other odds and ends, in the way of the wild West), but not much, and he didn't try to run that part of the operation directly. Mainly, he was a banker. On first arriving in Idaho from Colorado in 1887 he went to work as an assistant cashier at the Bank of Murray and later founded the Bank of North Idaho in that community. He was treasurer of Shoshone County for a couple of years. He sold his business in 1895, moved to Wallace, founded another bank, then moved to Boise to become cashier of the Boise City National Bank. He worked his way up in that organization and by 1916 was vice president; he would later become chairman of the board. He came to Idaho Power through its connection with the bank.

Johnson was not a very visible leader at Idaho Power, and mostly left the technicians alone. But, working out of an office that served him for both his banking and electric utility efforts, he got the new company on a sound financial footing. After all the financial and organizational conflict, he must have done a strong and effective job, because he remained as president from 1916 to 1931, and then stayed on as board chairman until 1935. By then, Idaho Power was solidly established, and ready to begin undertaking many of the major hydropower projects that have been its hallmark.

It seems like a steady progression in hindsight. But Frank Johnson probably would tell you it wasn't inevitable.

46 David THOMPSON

April 30, 1770 – February 10, 1857. Fur trader. Hope. Buried: Montreal, Quebec, Canada, Mount Royal Cemetery.

David Thompson is the one person on this list who never was a citizen or long-time resident of the United States, or even a long-time resident of Idaho. He was a native of England, and lived nearly all of his life in Canada spending only a quick stretch in what is now Idaho.

But his short time on the north shore of Lake Pend Oreille left reverberations that impacted the history of the area for decades to come. His time was commemorated in a monument at Hope which notes, "...the coming of the first white man to Lake Pend D'Oreille, David Thompson, explorer, geographer and fur trader."

Indentured in his youth to the Hudson's Bay Company, he learned about exploring and trading in furs, and traveled on foot distances that seem truly incredible. By 1801 he became a partner in the North West Company, exploring around Lake Superior north to the Slave Lake region in Canada. In 1806 (partly as a result, perhaps, of news of the American Lewis and Clark expedition?) he headed west, across the continental divide.

In 1809 he explored the upper Columbia area (now in British Columbia), then moved south, along Lake Pend Oreille, east of what is now Sandpoint. Here he paused – itself an unusual thing for a man who, as writer Cort Conley said, "moved like he had a posse on his tail." The spot on the lake, now called the Hope Peninsula, was at a useful juncture. It was easily accessible by water across an immense distance, and it was located at a crossroads near where a large number of tribal groups (the Flatheads, Spokans, Kalispels, Coeur d'Alenes) all lived. Here he set up the first commercial building in the Northwest by a person of European descent: Kullyspell House, a place where he and the various Indian groups all could trade among themselves. And it was used as such; there are indications the trading was brisk.

Exactly how long he stayed there we don't know. It wasn't long; he headed east down the Clark Fork to winter in what is now Montana. He probably resided in Idaho just about long enough to have (in modern terms) gotten a driver's license or qualified to vote – probably barely long enough to qualify for this list, and maybe less time than anyone else on it.

He returned to Lake Pend Oreille in the spring, stayed a short while, then headed east to sell the furs he had gathered. He may have visited the location once more (he would spend the remainder of his life in Canada), but Kullyspell House did not last long. It was abandoned after attacks from the Blackfeet, who were not part of the trading consortium and whose enemies had received rifles and other supplies from Thompson and his crew.

There was no direct follow-up to Thompson's short stay in Idaho. Kullyspell House was demolished, and even its location was unknown until a determined effort to locate it in 1923. Canadians never did move into the area, and people from the United States did not settled around Lake Pend Oreille until the 1880s.

So why is Thompson, remarkable as he may be, on this list?

One reason is Thompson's spectacular work as a geographer and mapmaker, filling in the gaps and explaining to the interested – and some key people *were* interested – what lay in what is now the upper Idaho Panhandle. (For years it was proprietary information of the North West Company, but the basic outlines undoubtedly made their way out over time.)

One of those interested persons surely was Father Pierre-Jean de Smet, whose deliberate travels through the region around 1840 had a big effect on the Coeur d'Alene Tribe and, indirectly, on United States settlement through the area. Thompson's story of establishing a prosperous trading center in the region must also have had some influence on later prospective settlers.

The secondary reason has to do with the pattern of settlement, and an answer to this question: If the prospects were so good, why did not the North West Company, and other Canadians, follow up? The answer probably has a lot to do with the relationships among the tribes in the area – especially the Blackfeet – which were affected by Thompson and his efforts at trading. Speculation is, word got out that, for a while at least, the area around Pend Oreille was not safe for Canadians. That may have helped clear the decks in the region for the United States settlers who arrived later.

47 C. Ben ROSS

December 27, 1876 – March 31, 1946. Farmer. Governor. Buried: Parma (near his homesite).

He was Idaho's first three-term governor, and one of the most colorful personalities ever in Idaho's political history – one reason he became one of the first, and for a long time one of the few, Idaho politicians to become the subject of a full-scale biography. If he seemed larger than life at the time, and once seemingly deserving of a place near the top of a list like this one, and now doesn't ...well, those facts all may have something to do with one another.

The first Idaho governor actually born in what is now the state (it was still Idaho Territory then), Ross was a Canyon County farmer for quite a few years before he moved east and started farm development in the Michaud Flats, in the Fort Hall area, which he helped pioneer. This sounds like the makings of a Republican politician, but Ross had a radical streak, and he spent years traveling the state, organizing farmers. He was an early founder of the Idaho Farm Bureau, ironically now considered a strongly Republican-based organization. During the tough twenties he was strongly identified with the "outs."

Ross served on the Canyon County commission from 1915-21, and was mayor of Pocatello from 1923-30. (One of the city's main parks is named for him.) Then in 1930 he was elected governor, and was re-elected twice, serving six years.

One reason he's on this list is what he did before becoming governor, during the depths of one of the weakest-ever periods for Idaho Democrats. The Democrats were weakened partly because many farmers were supporters of third-party interests, such as the

Nonpartisan League. Ross's biggest contribution was to woo them into the Democratic Party, using his powerful campaigning skill to couple that with support for the New Deal and for himself personally. In 1930 he broke the Democrats' decade-long losing streak for major office by winning the governorship; two years later the seeds he planted bore fruit, a massive, unprecedented Democratic across-the-board sweep, from congressional down to county offices.

Ross had a more ambitious view of government than the Republicans who ran Idaho government in the twenties. He made the first substantial expansions in Idaho government virtually since statehood, adding departments and staff. Much of that expanded government remained in the years that followed (owing in part to the advice proffered by Republican strategist Lloyd Adams, who happened to be close to Ross).

As governor, Ross oversaw reinstitution of direct primary elections, pushed through a state income tax (positioned as property tax relief), a kilowatt tax and an old-age pension law, and those achievements long outlasted him.

If Ross had sustained that effort he'd rank higher on this list. But he was an egotistical politician who allowed and sometimes fostered bitter conflicts within the ranks, and he built an impressive cadre of enemies. He often was combative. A mystic, convinced that his destiny was to be elected President, Ross lost sight of what was popular, proposing politically ruinous ideas such as a sales tax. That effort failed (dooming all similar efforts for another 30 years) and in 1936, in a battle against Sen. William Borah, Ross was crushed at the polls. He was never elected to anything again.

One could say that, before Ross and his Democratic organization self-destructed completely, the Democratic Party was partly absorbed by the quieter and more meticulous efforts of Tom Boise of Lewiston; so what Ross built was not completely destroyed. One could also point out that Ross was one of the first truly theatrical politicians in Idaho, paving the way later for people like Senator Glen Taylor (who was inspired by his example).

C. Ben Ross has to be assessed as a whale of a figure in Idaho in the thirties who might have been more.

48 Don CHANCE
Cal WILLIAMS

Don Chance: November 18, 1929 – March 30, 1992. Tax limitation advocate.

Cal Williams: January 19,1924 – July 7, 1992. Tax limitation advocate.

In early 1978, two California men unheard of a year earlier became two of the best-known names in the country: Howard Jarvis and Paul Gann. They were promoting a ballot initiative in California called "The Peoples Initiative to Limit Property Taxation," better known as Proposition 13. Their initiative was highly successful with California voters, passed at the polls on June 6, 1978, and set off a nationwide flurry of similar efforts to reduce or restrict property taxes.

In Idaho, two relatively unknown Boise businessmen, Don Chance and Cal Williams, took up the property tax limitation cause and formed the Idaho Property Owners Association. Although the organization never drew a significantly large statewide membership, its message caught on with Idaho voters, just as it had in California. Chance and Williams, both soft-spoken men, began circulating petitions to place an initiative on the 1978 Idaho general election ballot that would restrict property taxes to one percent of the property value, and that limited the property's growth in market value to two percent per year. In short order, they had enough signatures to place the issue on the election ballot.

Strong opposition developed from city and county government, public schools, fire and police organizations, and other public interests because the property tax was the major source of revenue supporting local services. But Chance and Williams did an excellent job of building public sentiment in support of the measure and in November it was approved. The measure had some serious legal conflicts with the Idaho constitution, but given the degree of voter support, representatives of the cities and schools were reluctant to mount too much of a challenge.

They instead worked closely and carefully with the Legislature to develop alternative statutes that, while keeping with the spirit of the initiative and restricting property tax increases, would still allow local government to continue to function, but considerable restrictions were placed on their ability to increase property taxes.

The success of Idaho's 1% Initiative would help launch other efforts in the future to place additional measures on the ballot further restricting the levying of property taxes in Idaho. But none of those efforts would succeed. Chance and Williams had come together in their effort and had found a perfect window of opportunity that has not occurred again.

Over the three decades following the 1978 1% Initiative success, local government has never been able to return to having the degree of control over levying taxes that they had prior to 1978.

But the 1% Initiative's impact on government funding actually extended far beyond limiting property taxes. In response to the initiative, state government began sharing state sales tax revenues with cities and counties. In addition, new or increased fees for various governmental services became commonplace. And the Legislature approved major shifts of public school funding away from the property tax and to state support.

Chance was born on November 18, 1929, at Smith Center Kansas. He served in the Army in both World War II and Korea. He moved to Idaho in 1946 and established an insurance agency that he ran until he retired. He died in Boise on March 30, 1992.

Williams was born on January 19, 1924, in Desdemona, Texas. Like Chance, he was a World War II veteran. He moved to Boise in 1963 and owned and operated Collister Lumber Company and Williams Realty. He passed away on July 7, 1992.

Chance and Williams probably had the greatest impact on Idaho's tax structure and the funding of government of any two individuals in the state's history.

49 | Frank STEUNENBERG

August 6, 1861 – December 30, 1905. Businessman, journalist. Governor. Buried: Caldwell, Canyon Hill Cemetery.

Frank Steunenberg is the guy whose statue is directly in front of, and faces, the Jefferson Street steps at the Idaho Statehouse, and who is best known for – as you'll find out if you ask about the statue – being blown up, assassinated by dynamite. That murder led to Idaho's most spectacular criminal trial, and it makes Steunenberg one of Idaho's most dramatic figures.

Politics junkies will note another curiosity about Steunenberg: No one ever has received a higher percentage of the vote for Idaho governor (79.79%). And Steunenberg, of Caldwell, was a Democrat.

But the man himself – was he personally all that pivotal?

He was, though in ways more subtle and less dramatic than the outsized factoids may suggest.

Steunenberg, with his brothers, was one of the founders of modern Caldwell, launching a newspaper, a bank, and a string of other businesses. He was a city council member and county auditor as well as a leader in the state Democratic Party, all in the decade leading up to his election as governor in 1896. He was not a great public speaker, but his breadth of experience and centrist inclinations positioned him neatly to take advantage of a perfect political storm. In brief: The depression of the early 1890s caused three major splinters in what was the strong Republican coalition that had operated in Idaho at the point of statehood. Mining interests wanted the price of silver propped up, and "Silver Republicans" (who in Idaho included William Borah and Fred T. Dubois) split from the main stem Republicans over it. Mining labor had split as well, and many of their candidates ran as Populists; so did candidates of a number of agricultural activists. In 1896 Steunenberg drew the support of not only traditional Democrats, but also the Populists and the Silver Republicans. It was a political shift in Idaho of enormous magnitude, and for a couple of years it seemed likely to reshape the state. Steunenberg was the central figure who made it possible locally – for a short time.

He also was the central figure who blasted it apart locally. Labor activists in the Silver Valley, pushing harder against the anti-union Bunker Hill mine, sought support from Steunenberg, asking for example that a couple of state national guard units stationed to protect mine property be dismissed. Steunenberg declined, and proceeded over the next couple of years to seriously misread – both overestimating and underestimating – the nature of labor unrest in the Silver Valley. He eventually called for federal troops, which made the conflict there even worse. Steunenberg, originally seen by labor as a good friend (he had once been a typographical union member himself), was now seen as a turncoat. (That emotional reaction to him was the genesis of his 1906 assassination by labor activist Harry Orchard.) The alliance of 1896 collapsed in part when Steunenberg narrowly won a second term in 1898, and entirely by 1900 when he was crushed in a bid for the U.S. Senate.

The political dominance the Idaho Republican Party began to put in place early in the 20th century owed much to its own coalition of forces—but something also to the fact that Democrats had such a hard time, for a period of decades, putting together farm and labor alliances, as did happen in a number of other states. A large part of the reason in Idaho can be traced to the Steunenberg years.

50 Calvin COBB

July 15, 1853 – November 7, 1928. Newspaper publisher. Boise. Buried

Since the earliest territorial days, as the old slogan long had it, the *Idaho Statesman* (once the *Tri-Weeky Statesman* and later the *Daily Statesman*) genuinely has been "part of life in Idaho." It has gone through few truly major changes in all that time, starting life as a Republican newspaper and moving to a relatively independent stance in the last generation.

No such centrist efforts were made until well into the twentieth century. Newspapers in the Gilded Age and the Progressive Era were overtly partisan and very much attached to power structures, whether in or out of power, in their local areas. For many decades, the *Statesman* was an integral part of the Idaho Republican power structure, and for a long time the man in charge of that part of the machinery was Calvin Cobb – the Idaho "chancellor of Republican politics," as one eastern Idaho observer put it.

Cobb, born in Cleveland, grew up in Chicago in a book publishing family. (It helped give him entrée in upper-crust social circles around the country.) He struck out briefly in the cattle business, but when an 1886 trip west took him to Boise, he stayed. With his brother-in-law, and probably help from family money, he gained control of the *Idaho Daily Statesman*.

The paper had just reached the age of 22, and was, as in most cities then, just one of several papers. Cobb over time maneuvered to control and eventually wipe out most of the opposition. By the new century only the *Capital News* remained; it would last until 1942; but while nominally a Democratic paper Cobb and allied Republicans bought what amounted to effective control of it – keeping it on a leash. From before 1900, Boise was for most practical purposes a one-paper town well before the day when that was standard, and that one paper was solidly Republican in outlook. Calvin Cobb was the central reason. The transition of the Boise area to solidly Republican in orientation was also clearly influenced by Cobb as well. He was a prime early promoter of William Borah, though they split when Borah adopted a pro-silver position that divided him from the mainstem of the Republican Party.

After Cobb died in 1928, his daughter Margaret Cobb Ailshie took over as the Statesman publisher, and she held that job until 1959. She maintained her father's policies at the paper, directed by general manager James Brown, who in turn led the paper into 1963, when it was sold to Federated Newspapers (the first in a series of chain sales). That meant Cobb's basic ideas stayed in place at the *Statesman* for more than three-fourths of a century.

He also put in place, however, a transition toward the more modern, non-partisan, approach in news gathering. Cobb was highly active in the Associated Press (and its development in Idaho), becoming national vice chair of the cooperative, and the AP's approach to news took hold, over time, at the *Statesman*.

Elias D. Pierce/2

Charles Rich/35

Lawyer/33

Moses Splawn/28, with neice Lallooh

David Ballard/63

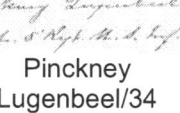
Pinckney Lugenbeel/34

Hill Beachey/96

C.W. Moore/24

IDAHO 100

John Neil/82

William Dewey/41

James Guffey/38

Thomas Ricks/8

Aaron Parker/78

William Budge/13

Drew Standrod/44

Fred Dubois/9

Edward Stevenson/17

Richard Z. Johnson/97

James Hawley/40

George Shoup/89

William Clagett/4

Ira B. Perrine/3

James Ailshie/6

Alfred Budge/73

William McConnell/93

Frank Steunenberg/49

 Tom Roach/7
 Len Jordan/95
 Robert Smylie/18

 John R. Simplot/11

 Ezra Taft Benson/27
 Verda Barnes/65 (with Frank Church)

IDAHO 100 125

Joe Albertson/19

Cecil Andrus/16 (left) and Frank Church/14

James McClure/23

John Evans/76 (and Claire Moncrief)

James Taylor/67

Harry Magnuson/57

Perry Swisher/72

Charles McDevitt/77

Photo credits

Elias Pierce (origin unknown)
Charles Rich (Illustrated History of the State of Idaho)
Lawyer (Credit: Edward S. Curtis; Library of Congress)
Moses Splawn (with niece Lallooh about 1921. Permission of Dr. Eric Splawn)
David Ballard (Library of Congress)
Pinckney Lugenbeel (origin unknown, widely distributed on Internet)
Hill Beachy (from a newspaper clipped, publication and date unknown)
CW Moore (By permission of the Moore-Bettis Family.)
John Neil (taken from a 1900-era Idaho history, title unknown)
William Dewey (Illustrated History of the State of Idaho)
James Guffey (Memoirs of Allegheny County, PA., Northwestern Historical Association (1904))
Thomas Ricks (Credit Church of Jesus Christ of Latter Day Saints)
Aaron Parker (courtesy Paul Engstrom)
William Budge (Illustrated History of the State of Idaho)
Drew Standrod (H.T. French History of Idaho)
Fred Dubois (Library of Congress)
Edward Stevenson (originally from the American Monthly Review of Reviews)
Edward Stevenson (ML Peterson collection)
Richard Johnson (An Illustrated History of Idaho)
James Hawley (Library of Congress)
George Shoup (M.L. Peterson collection)
William Clagett (Library of Congress)
IB Perrine (from out-of-copyright book "The Potato" by Grubb and Gillford 1912.)
James Ailshie (courtesy University of Idaho library)
Alfred Budge (H.T. French History of Idaho)
William McConnell (W. J. McConnell, Early History of Idaho)
Frank Steunenberg (ML Peterson collection)

IDAHO 100

Frank Gooding (Library of Congress)
Bill Haywood (Library of Congress)
William Deary (courtesy University of Idaho library)
John Hailey (John Hailey, History of Idaho)
Moses Alexander (Illustrated History of the State of Idaho)
William Borah (Library of Congress)
Lloyd Adams (from the Upper Snake River Historical Society, Rexburg)
Joe Marshall (from the Beale-Wells History of Idaho JUDY)
C.A. Robins (ML Peterson collection)
Tom Roach (Idaho Power Company)
Len Jordan (ML Peterson collection)
Robert Smylie (permission of Steve Smylie)
JR Simplot (JR Simplot Company)
Ezra Taft Benson (Credit Church of Jesus Christ of Latter Day Saints)
Verda Barnes (with Frank Church; M.L. Peterson collection)
Joe Albertson (Albertson's)
Cecil Andrus/Frank Church (M.L. Peterson)
James McClure (courtesy University of Idaho library)
John Evans w/Claire Moncrief (M.L. Peterson)
James Taylor (courtesy College of Southern Idaho)
Harry Magnuson (Idaho Centennial Commission)
Perry Swisher (Idaho Public Utilities Commission)
Charles McDevitt (Idaho Supreme Court)

51 William Judson BOONE

November 5, 1860 – July 8, 1936. Minister. Caldwell.

A native of Pennsylvania, William Judson Boone studied religion at the College of Wooster in Ohio, received his divinity degree from Western Theological Seminary in Pittsburgh, and, that done, headed west to his first job as a Presbyterian minister. He stepped off the train at Caldwell, Idaho, and went to work.

It turned out to be more than that, though his ministerial job lasted only six years. In 1891 he helped found and became the first president of The College of Idaho at Caldwell.

The college did not start off with a bang: There were just seven faculty members, and only two students in the first year. But it grew.

The C of I was founded as a Presbyterian institution it still has ties to the Presbyterian Church but is no longer a denominational institution), and when it was founded it was the first private college in Idaho. Ricks College, planted three years earlier, called itself an academy until 1918; and even the University of Idaho, the first public university, was only two years old then. A forceful figure, Boone made the new Caldwell institution work almost through force of will, and through a series of outside endowments and contributions he was able to obtain over the years.

Any college is an important element of its community, but The College of Idaho may have outsized impact in Idaho considering its relatively small size.

Its moderate tone seems not to have greatly influenced the politics or culture of Caldwell, which have remained conservative and resource industry-oriented over the years, but it has had a significant impact on Idaho overall through the decades. Its alumni and close associates include a number of people on this list, such as Joe Albertson and Robert Smylie, both of whom gave back to the institution in their later years.

Boone's many activities in Idaho ranged far beyond the C of I and Caldwell. He planted numerous other churches around Idaho, and influenced communities across the state in the process. He was one of Idaho's foremost religious figures in his time. On a different level, his highly skilled photographic work has preserved the visual history of campus, community, and region, and his equal skills as a botanist contributed to understanding of the landscape of the area.

52 William D. HAYWOOD

February 4, 1869 – May 18, 1928. Union leader. Boise, Silver City. Buried: partly in Moscow, Russia, in the Kremlin wall, partly in Chicago, Illinois, near the Haymarket Martyr's Monument.

For a short period, William "Big Bill" Haywood may have had a greater impact on more United States citizens than any other person with Idaho roots. Only the Revolutionary and Civil wars created greater levels of internal conflict in the United States than Haywood's efforts at fomenting class warfare in the early part of the twentieth century.

Bill Haywood was born in Salt Lake City on April 4, 1869. At the age of fifteen, he went to work as a miner at the Ohio mine in Humboldt County, Nevada. When that mine closed, he tried his hand, without success, at cowboying and homesteading. In 1894, Haywood found himself unemployed with a wife and child. He decided to go north to Silver City, Idaho, in search of employment in the mines there.

He landed a job in the Blaine mine, and there he first heard stories about labor unrest in the coal mines of Pennsylvania and the battles between the Molly Maguires (a secret society of coal miners) and the Pinkerton detectives. In June of that year, as he was working in the mine, he was involved in an accident that nearly cost him one of his hands. Shortly after that, while Haywood was unable to work with his arm in a sling, Edward Boyce, the president of the Western Federation of Miners, visited Silver City. Haywood attended two meetings conducted by Boyce in an effort to recruit members to the union. He was impressed with Boyce's message. So were several hundred other miners who signed up to form Silver City Miners Union Number 66 of the Western Federation of Miners.

Haywood became an active union member, soon treasurer, then president of the local. He also worked actively to recruit members until it had more than 1,000 members. Haywood worked hard on behalf of his members; among other things, the union had its own hospital – the only hospital in the Owyhee country.

In 1898 Haywood was elected a delegate to the Western Federation of Miners Convention in Salt Lake City. He had his first opportunity to mix with miners from other locations who shared similar interests. He also met, for the first time, miners who had been part of the labor troubles in the Coeur d'Alenes in 1892. He came away greatly impressed and was elected to the federation's executive board. In his new role, he spent time in the Coeur d'Alenes as an organizer, and also at Rocky Bar. He also began writing articles for the IWW's *Miners' Magazine*.

Haywood became the number-two leader in the Western Federation of Miners, a founder and leader of the Industrial Workers of the World (the "wobblies"), and a member of the executive committee of the Socialist Party of America. Haywood and his cohorts seldom shied away from violent conflicts, in fact preferring direct action over political solutions. He may have been involved with orchestrating the 1906 assassination of former Idaho Governor Frank Steunenberg. In 1907, Haywood was kidnapped from Denver and brought to Boise to stand trial for conspiracy in that murder, along with others from the Western Federation of Miners. During what was termed the Trial of the Century (his defense lawyer was Clarence Darrow), the focus of much of the country was on Boise. None of those charged with conspiracy in the murder was convicted, although suspicions about Haywood's involvement in particular persist. Harry Orchard, who actually set the bomb, pled guilty and spent the rest of his long life at the Idaho State Penitentiary.

Haywood continued his promotion of radical causes and in 1918 was convicted of violating the Espionage Act of 1917. He fled to the new Russian Socialist Federative Republic, where he joined the Communist Party and spent his remaining years as an occasionally useful front-person for Lenin. He died from a stroke on May 18, 1928, while living in Moscow. At his request, half of his ashes were buried in the Kremlin Wall and the other half alongside victims of the Haymarket riots in Chicago.

53 Permeal FRENCH

May 8, 1869 – October 10, 1954. Educator. Superintendent of Public Instruction. Buried: Hailey, family plot.

Permeal Jane French was the first native-born Idaho woman to rise to statewide prominence. She did it without the assistance of a wealthy family or a well-placed husband.

French was born in Idaho City. The exact date is slippery; May 8, 1869 is often cited, but dates from 1866 to 1870 have been noted, and her headstone says 1867. She attended elementary school in Idaho City and high school at the Academy of Notre Dame, a Catholic school in San Francisco.

After graduation, she moved to Bellevue, Idaho, where her widowed mother ran a boarding house. In 1892, she took her first stab at state government, becoming a journal clerk in the Idaho Senate for $5 a day. In 1895, she was hired as a teacher at the public school in Hailey, even though she didn't have a teaching certificate (not a big issue in those days).

French moved to Silver City in 1896 and became a popular teacher and a significant part of the social scene. There was even a rumor that she had become engaged to Captain Joseph DeLamar, a successful local mine owner and state senator. But Silver City had more to offer. This was a time when many of Idaho's most significant figures either lived in Silver City or had a connection to the town. They included William E. Borah, a Boise attorney who represented a number of Silver City clients, and Governor Frank Steunenberg. Those connections helped her enter politics.

In 1898, she decided to run for State Superintendent of Public Instruction. It was a risky move, since no woman had ever been elected to statewide office in Idaho before. But she was a Democrat, and there was growing support for the Democratic Party in Idaho. In addition, she had established a network of politically influential friends. In the election, she ran on both the Democratic and Populist party tickets and was elected. In fact she was one of two Silver City residents elected to statewide office in that election. The other was the manager of the Trade Dollar Mine, Joe Hutchison, who was elected lieutenant governor.

She served two terms as Superintendent of Public Instruction, and her accomplishments were significant. She successfully sponsored legislation that gave the superintendent control over a wide range of standards, including curriculum. Today you can visit her old school in Silver City and see a sign outside the building proclaiming it an "Idaho Standard School." She drafted a new education code that required teacher exams and certificates. The reforms she pushed were somewhat revolutionary for the time and they formed the basis for Idaho's modern public school structure.

French was turned out of office in 1902 in a Republican sweep. After a brief sojourn at homesteading the Bellevue area, she was asked by the University of Idaho to become their first dean of women. She would serve there for the next thirty years.

French was an administrator, disciplinarian, and humanitarian. She also became the guiding force for several generations of both women and men attending the university. When she determined that the university, with no student union building, needed a place for students to gather socially, she used her own money to build the Blue Bucket Inn. The name was perhaps a reminder of her days in Silver City, where the original mining strikes were by a party looking for the legendary Lost Blue Bucket Mine.

Former Idaho first lady Grace Jordan once wrote a piece about French entitled "The Woman Who Made Ladies and Gentlemen." A biography is entitled "*Dowager of Discipline*." She may have had more impact on young people of that era than any other Idahoan.

When she retired in 1939 at age seventy, the university paid her $21,200 for the Blue Bucket Inn. In retirement she moved to Seattle where she died on October 10, 1954. The previous day the university's Board of Regents had sent her a telegram informing her that they were naming a new women's dormitory after her.

54 | John HAINES

January 1, 1863 – June 4, 1917. Real estate developer. Governor. Boise. Buried: Boise, Morris Hill Cemetery.

If latter-day Idahoans are given a description of Governor John Haines, who was elected to one term in 1912, as a successful real estate developer and a Republican politician who proclaimed that government should be small and austere and taxes should be kept low, they would probably peg him as a familiar political type from a century later. And he was all that. But he's on this list because he was a good deal more as well.

An Iowa native, Haines spent his early adulthood dealing real estate in Kansas, only to be wiped out by a severe drought in the late 1890s. Along with many others, he headed west, to Idaho. On the way, he encountered several other would-be realtors, and when they got to Boise they formed the W.E. Pierce and Company real estate firm. It rapidly became the leading realty firm in Idaho, and played an important role in the development of southwest Idaho—Boise in particular. That development became all the more important because the senior partner, W.E. Pierce, was elected Boise mayor in 1903, and Haines succeeded him in 1907.

The office of mayor gave Haines the platform to run for governor in 1912, in a race he only barely won over Democrat James Hawley, after running hard on a campaign of fiscal austerity.

He turned out, once elected, to have a head for reform, in all sorts of areas. He pushed for non-partisan election of judges (who then ran on party tickets; his suggestion would be taken after a few years). He pressed for the full range of progressive political issues, including the recall and referendum. Governing during a session when legislators were preoccupied with choosing a new U.S. senator, he argued for passage of the 17th amendment to turn that over to the voters. And, amid the political confusion, he became central in the 1913 session in setting an agenda for passing what he considered very important items. He got them.

One was creation of a state Board of Education. Idaho already had a board of regents for the University of Idaho, but the new board would be united with it and oversee education statewide. That same system survives a century later.

So has Haines's proposal for a public utility commission. He pushed the idea at a time when electric power companies were just starting to merge, when other utilities were beginning to turn into larger companies. Idaho presumably would have wound up regulating them in some fashion in later years; but if it had been done at a point when utility lobbyists became much more powerful, the regulatory structure might have looked a lot different.

He also proposed creating the Workman's Compensation Board (later, and currently, the Industrial Commission), which is still active in essentially the same form.

Haines was a close watcher of the legislature, proposing and vetoing with great frequency (and sometimes even vetoing bills that grew out of his proposals). The counties of Gooding, Franklin, Jefferson, Minidoka, and Power were created in 1913, with his explicit approval. He vetoed creation of Valley County by splitting Boise County, however, saying the change would leave Boise County with too little valuation. That would have to wait another few years.

In all, Haines' two years as governor marked one of the most critical legislative periods in Idaho history. It was not enough for a re-election, however. A scandal in the treasurer's office, over which Haines had no control, has been thought to be one reason why; another may be that the Democratic winner, Moses Alexander, another Boise mayor, was a particularly strong candidate.

55 Willis SWEET

January 1, 1856 – July 9, 1925. Attorney. U.S. Representative. Buried: Mayaguez, Puerto Rico, Santurce Cemetery.

Credit for placing the University of Idaho at Moscow and the state penitentiary at Boise has been variously attributed, and belongs to more than one person. Willis Sweet probably stands foremost among them.

Sweet, a Vermont native, was one of the leading figures in Idaho Republican politics at the time of statehood, and he became the new state's first member of the U.S. House, serving two terms. (He lost a bid for the Senate in 1896.) After his time in Congress he moved to Coeur d'Alene to practice law, and in 1903 he moved to Puerto Rico to become attorney general there.

But his more significant roles came earlier.

Sweet moved to Moscow in 1881 as a printer, read law and was admitted to the bar; by 1888 he was well enough regarded to be named U.S. attorney for Idaho, and the next year he became an Idaho Supreme Court justice. He was also a member of the territorial legislature, and in 1888 he and a representative from Genesee, J.W. Brigham, sponsored and pushed through legislation to declare Moscow the home of the future University of Idaho. The university was officially created on that basis in January 1889.

When time came for choosing delegates to a state constitutional convention, he was a natural, and he quickly became one of the leading figures. Among other actions there, he helped craft language that built the University of Idaho's location and status into the Idaho Constitution.

More sweepingly, Sweet was the leading convention link to the then most influential political figure in Idaho, Fred T. Dubois, who was then busy pushing Idaho statehood through Congress. Their alliance was one of the subtle pressures on the convention, made easier by Sweet's informal role as chief public spokesman for the majority Republican caucus at the convention. After William Clagett, he may have been the most effective single shaper of the final document.

56 Lynn DRISCOLL

May 3, 1891 – March 9, 1977. Banker. Boise. Buried: Boise, Morris Hill Cemetery.

There could have been few challenges to equal being a banker during the Great Depression – especially if you had moved to Idaho to become president of a bank just before the Wall Street crash of October 1929.

John Lynn Driscoll, Sr., was such a person. He was born in Craig, Nebraska, on May 3, 1891, and in 1905 moved with his family to Boise, where his father began work for an investment and real estate firm. Following graduation from Boise High School in 1910, he enrolled at the University of Nebraska and graduated in 1914. His first job out of college was with the Overland National Bank in Grand Island, Nebraska. Moving to Chicago in 1915, he worked for the Live Stock Exchange National Bank and then as vice president of the Boise Live Stock Company of Chicago.

In 1929, nineteen years after he had left Boise, he returned as president of the First Security Bank of Boise. This bank was part of a newly formed group of banks in Utah, Idaho, and Wyoming owned by the Eccles family of Salt Lake and E.G. Bennett of Idaho Falls. The banks were organized under a holding company called the First Security Corporation, thought to be the first multi-bank holding company in the United States.

The three major banks in Idaho in 1932 were Boise City National, First National Bank of Idaho and First Security Bank of Boise. By August both Boise City and First National had closed their doors. Although First Security remained open, Driscoll sensed there would soon be a run on it and ordered $1 million in cash from the Federal Reserve Bank in Salt Lake City.

On the morning of August 31, crowds were lined up at the door of the bank waiting for it to open so they could withdraw their funds. He told the tellers to politely meet all demands and that, in recognition of the Western Idaho Fair, the bank would close at noon. But then he changed his mind and had a sign painter paint a sign saying "For the benefit of our patrons This Bank Will Be OPEN UNTIL LATE TONIGHT. If You Want Your Money Come and Get It." The sign and the offer it contained comforted most of the customers and the bank remained open until 9:00 p.m., surviving the panic.

In 1933, First Security's Idaho holdings were merged into the First Security Bank of Idaho, with Driscoll first serving as executive vice president and then president. First Security quickly became one of the largest banking chains in Idaho, taking an active role in supporting the personal and commercial banking needs of thousands of Idahoans.

Driscoll became widely known, not only as Idaho's premier banker of the day, but also as a community leader. He was president of the Boise Chamber of Commerce in 1929 and was on the Boise school board for eight years, followed by seven years as president of the board of trustees of Boise Junior College. Drawing on his experience with the Boise Live Stock Company, he served as head of the Idaho Sheep Commission in the 1920s and as a director of the Children's Home Society. He was also politically active. When William E. Borah sought the Republican presidential nomination in 1936, Driscoll was elected a delegate to the Republican National Convention.

Driscoll collaborated with historian Glen Barrett on a book about his life titled "*J. Lynn Driscoll: Western Banker.*" The book came out in 1974. He had made much of that history, as one of the central figures involved in modernizing banks and bringing branch banking to Idaho.

57 H.F. "Harry" MAGNUSON

March 14, 1923 – January 24, 2009. Accountant. Buried:

The most important things in Harry Magnuson's life took place within the city limits of Wallace. It was where he was born, went to school, met his wife, raised his family, and had his office. In turn, Wallace as a viable city might not exist but for Magnuson.

But his influence extended far beyond the Wallace city limits.

He was born on March 14, 1923. Despite his Scandinavian surname, his heritage was strongly Italian. His mother's family immigrated to the Silver Valley from Italy. Harry's maternal grandfather was one of the hundreds of miners who were rounded up and imprisoned in the makeshift prison called the bullpen during the 1899 labor confrontations in the Coeur d'Alenes that focused on low wages paid by the Bunker Hill mine. As a result, Magnuson's grandfather was banned from ever returning to work in the mines.

After service in the Navy in World War II, Magnuson received a degree in business from the University of Idaho and then his MBA from Harvard. After a short stint as an accountant for Hecla Mining Company, he established his own accounting firm. He also began investing in mining stocks and real estate. Over the years those investment grew until he had major interests in mining, banking, shopping centers, a newspaper, hotels, and real estate. With his success in mining ventures, he became known in the news media as "Idaho mining magnate H. F. Magnuson." Among other things, he was on the boards of Hecla, Golconda Mining, and Bunker Hill and was president of the Silver Dollar Mining Co. He also served on the boards of General Telephone and Albertsons for many years.

Magnuson used his accumulating wealth and influence to support a wide range of public interests. For many years he fought to keep the interstate highway from bisecting Wallace. In the end, the interstate was routed along the edge of the city and the historic downtown business area preserved. The main street artery through Wallace is now known as Harry Magnuson Way, wordplay on the idea that Harry Magnuson usually got his way. Former Governor Cecil Andrus remarked at the time of Magnuson's death, "The city of Wallace would have disappeared off the face of the map if it hadn't been for Harry Magnuson."

When the Bunker Hill and Sullivan Mine was closed, he put together a limited partnership with two other Idaho business giants, J.R. Simplot and Duane Hagadone, and purchased the mine in what would eventually prove to be an unsuccessful effort to put the facility back into operation.

He was also a deeply religious Catholic who served for many years on the board of trustees of Gonzaga University in Spokane. When Gonzaga ran into serious financial difficulties and was threatened with closure in the late 1960s, Magnuson personally guaranteeing the loans necessary to keep it operating.

One of his other great passions was Idaho history. Whether it was the preservation of the Old Mission at Cataldo, or the development of a museum in Wallace, he could be counted on to make full use of his connections and resources in support of the effort. When Idaho celebrated its statehood centennial in 1990, he served as chairman of the Idaho Centennial Commission. As the largest private land owner on Lake Coeur d'Alene, he made it possible for the Coeur d'Alene Indian tribe to buy from him, at a "fire sale" price, tracts that had historically been tribal lands.

When Harry Maguson died on January 24, 2009, two funeral services were held, one in Wallace and the other at Gonzaga University, each reflecting places important to Magnuson's life. The Gonzaga service featured a funeral mass conducted by nineteen Jesuit priests and the Catholic bishop of Idaho, as well as a ceremony by members of the Coeur d'Alene Indian tribe.

58 Georgia DAVIDSON

May 18, 1908 – April 6, 1997. Radio-TV station owner.

If anyone could qualify as a pioneer Idaho broadcaster, Georgia Davidson surely would. She brought television to Idaho, founded its still-dominant local station, and provided critical early fostering help for Idaho Public Television.

She grew up on a ranch in western Canyon County; her father was elected to the Idaho Senate in 1932 from that county. She attended the University of Oregon, where she met C.J. Phillips. She was the piano accompanist for a quartet that included Phillips, and their live radio programs were her first broadcasting experience. She and Phillips were married in 1927; the next year they moved to Boise where they bought southern Idaho's oldest radio station, KFAU, from the Boise Independent School District. It was not then much of a radio station; it had been founded as an extremely low-wattage high school station, intended mainly to give the students a look at (and chance to work with) the equipment. The Phillipses changed the call letters to KIDO, and made it a professional operation. It was southwestern Idaho's first commercial, and first viable, radio station.

C.J. Phillips died unexpectedly in 1946 and Davidson became the sole owner of the station. With her experience in every aspect of managing the station, from custodial work to writing commercial copy to selling advertising, she turned KIDO into a highly successful operation.

She was one of the few women in radio management. Four years after Phillips died, she married Boise businessman R. Mowbray Davidson.

It was in television that Georgia Davidson would firmly establish herself as a leading broadcast executive. Sensing that the fledgling industry had great potential, she applied for a license for a Boise station, and it was granted in December 1952. On July 12, 1953, KIDO-TV, Idaho's first television station and an NBC affiliate, signed on for the first time. It was 105 degrees outside. Present at the inaugural broadcast were Philo Farnsworth, an Idaho native known as the father of television, Idaho governor Len Jordan and Boise mayor R. E. Edlefsen.

The station went on the air just as the 1953 recession hit. Davidson had borrowed $350,000 to put the station on the air, with KIDO radio as the collateral. She sold the radio station, even though it was making money and the TV station was in the red, because she believed in TV.

In 1956, the station brought the first live telecast to Idaho when it broadcast the World Series.

Unlike many commercial broadcasters, Davidson was also a champion of public television. In 1967, she arranged for her satellite station in La Grande, Oregon, to receive a live broadcast from the University of Idaho's KUID-TV, and relay it to Boise where it was re-broadcast by KTVB. Before Boise's public television station, KAID, went on the air in 1971, she pre-empted the second hour of the Today Show so that KTVB could carry Sesame Street on weekday mornings without commercial interruptions. Idaho Public Television got an earlier and stronger start in Idaho than it might have without her.

In 1979, with KTVB at the top of the ratings in Idaho, both with its NBC network programming and its local news broadcasts, Davidson sold KTVB to the Bullitt family's KING Broadcasting headquartered in Seattle. At this writing, it has remained the ratings leader in Idaho for decades.

Georgia Davidson died in Boise on April 6, 1997 at age 89. In her later years she was quoted as saying that she had become disappointed in television entertainment with its emphasis on sex, violence, and guns. She viewed television as a miracle and believed that it deserved better.

59 Michael JORDAN

March 17, 1832 – July 11, 1864. Miner. Delamar. Buried: Rural Owyhee County, unmarked grave.

Michael Jordan's life could have been made into a John Ford western movie. His story had it all: Covered wagons, shootouts, steamboats, prospectors, ranchers, Indians.

Jordan was born in Ontario, Canada, on March 17, 1832. In 1842 his family moved across the border to Wisconsin. Seven years later at age seventeen, he left home and joined a wagon train headed to the gold fields of California. He prospected in a number of areas before he formed the Placerville Mining Company. He continued to prospect and eventually teamed up with William H. Dewey, who, within a few years, would become one of Idaho's wealthiest citizens. By 1862, he and Dewey were in Virginia City, Nevada, and had lost everything. Jordan departed to seek his fortune in the Pacific Northwest. Spending the winter of 1862-63 in Walla Walla, he met a group of men who had been part of the Grimes Party that discovered gold in the Boise Basin several months earlier. They were obtaining supplies and preparing to return to the Boise Basin. Jordan joined their party.

In the Boise Basin, Jordan found that most of the land had already been staked out with mining claims. Intent on prospecting, he formed a party of 29 men and 60 horses and mules and departed to the unexplored territory south of the Snake River. They crossed the river and traveled south into the Owyhee Mountains. Camping at a spot near the current town site of Delamar, they began panning for gold. Soon, all members of the party were successful in finding gold.

They called the stream Jordan Creek, after Michael Jordan. Soon word spread back to the Boise Basin and the area was inundated with prospectors, most of whom left disappointed when they discovered that the 29 members of the Jordan Party had staked out claims to most of the land in the area. The members of the original party spent the rest of the year prospecting.

By 1864, "float boulders" of high grade silver ore had been discovered further upstream near what is now Silver City. This led to a frenzy of mining activity as prospectors attempted to find the sources of the silver ore in the surrounding mountains. The Owyhee mines quickly attracted international attention, and investors from across the U.S. and Europe hoped to make their fortunes there. For a period of time, the Owyhees were one of the most productive mining areas in the United States. In addition, the opening of the Owyhee mines also opened up much of southern Idaho to settlement as transportation links were created between the mines and Nevada, California, and Oregon.

Jordan also partnered in developing a toll road and a ranch in the area. On July 11, 1864, Indians stole a number of horses and mules from Jordan. He and Silver City businessman Hosea Eastman formed a party to pursue the Indians and reclaim the stolen stock. During the ensuing battle, Jordan was killed. The next day a group of 120 men returned to the battle site and recovered Jordan's dismembered body. It was buried nearby in an unmarked grave.

As a result of Michael Jordan's prospecting and discoveries in the Owyhees, the region prospered for a time and attracted people who would go on to become cornerstones of the Boise business community and some of Idaho's most successful and effective politicians.

60   Clifford J. STRIKE

April 11, 1895 – February 11, 1948. Utility executive. Buried: Cloverdale Memorial Park, Boise.

Clifford Strike was the fourth president and chairman of Idaho Power Company—and in many ways the most pivotal of any in the company's history. He set the company firmly on the road to hydropower development, bringing in cheap power that allowed for the coming growth in Idaho. He also reorganized the company to give the independence it has had since.

Strike's electric power career started modestly, as a lineman working in the plains states. His management abilities must have been recognized early on, because by 1938 he was president of a South Dakota electric utility. That year Idaho Power Company recruited him, its first outside hire for president. He would be president and chairman until 1947, just months before his death.

When he was hired, Idaho Power was still controlled by Electric Bond and Share, a holding company that had created the utility in 1916 from a merger of several smaller companies. EBS also had a string of other electric utility companies around the country.

The Holding Company Act of 1935 limited (especially geographically) the properties that holding companies could keep. In Idaho Power's and EBS's case, figuring out what would happen next involved years of negotiation and sifting. Strike was the central figure on Idaho Power's side; he led the company to independence in September 1943, when it went public.

Going public meant an infusion of cash, and Strike swiftly put it to use. As soon as World War II ended, the Idaho Power history

Hydro Era recounts, "Idaho Power commenced an expansion program of unprecedented proportions. Within a six-year period, the company was to build six power plants to near quadruple capacity. Blueprints pointed to Hagerman Valley to increase generation at three sites. A diversion canal at Upper Salmon falls would be extended from units one and two to power a new plant, units three and four. This project launched underway in the fall of 1945. The company had launched a multi-million dollar expansion."

Strike lived just long enough to see one of the projects completed, but all were well underway by the time he resigned as president.

He is the namesake of yet another project (also on his planning table), completed about four years after his death – the C.J. Strike Dam near Bruneau.

In early 1947, Strike reached out to an old acquaintance from South Dakota, Thomas Roach, then president of Northwestern Electric Company in Portland, Oregon, and persuaded him to come to Idaho Power, to succeed him – as Roach did only months later. Roach, also on this list, proved to be one of the key figures in the history not only of Idaho Power but also of Idaho.

61 Erwin GRAUE

1895 – April 21, 1994. University professor.

Erwin Graue, a professor of economics at the University of Idaho, was once described as "a crusty old freemarketer." As such he became a major influence on generations of students whose careers included everything from corporate executive to the church historian for the LDS Church, including many of the people who decades would constitute Idaho's leadership.

Graue was born in Germany in 1895 – he never lost his German accent – and emigrated to the United States after World War I, in 1918. He graduated from Cornell University and then began additional studies at the New School of Social Research in New York while collaborating with economists at the University of Chicago. He received his Ph.D. in economics from Cornell University in 1928 and then accepted a position as an assistant professor of economics at the University of Idaho. It was the beginning of a 37-year career at the university; in the course of it, he cast a lifelong influence on hundreds, if not thousands, of students who passed through his classes.

His specialties were economic statistics, business, and agricultural economics, the sort of course work needed to help prepare students for the business world in Idaho and elsewhere. He also took a strong personal interest in his students that often extended beyond the classroom. During World War II, he regularly wrote letters to his former students serving in the military, providing them with news from the University of Idaho and cheering them up; they responded by providing whatever news they were allowed to communicate from the front.

Business executives from Idaho and elsewhere have given Dr. Graue major credit for launching them on their successful careers. One of his earliest students was A.D. Davis, who graduated in 1929 and went on to co-found Winn-Dixie, which would eventually own more than 1,000 supermarkets. Other former students became CEOs or senior executives with such firms as Morrison-Knudsen, Boeing, Boise Cascade, Merrill-Lynch, Albertson's, Texaco, and U.S. Steel.

In addition to influencing future corporate executives, he had a major influence on individuals who would serve in the U.S. Senate, the Idaho Supreme Court, and the Idaho Legislature.

Perhaps his most lasting and ongoing impact was with the creation of the Public Utilities Executives Course at the university. For more than fifty years this course has been a training ground for utility executives from throughout the United States and the world.

The University of Idaho had a mandatory retirement age of seventy. In 1965, Graue retired from the University of Idaho and moved on to Gonzaga University, where he taught for another twenty-one years. When he retired from Gonzaga, the university created an endowed faculty chair in his name, which was primarily funded by former University of Idaho students. More recently, the University of Idaho has established a Graue Scholars program in his name.

Erwin Graue died on April 21, 1994, at the age of ninety-nine.

62 Bill CAMPBELL

March 10, 1922 – July 13, 2001. Insurance executive, political activist, sports enthusiast.

Bill Campbell's rise in Idaho Republican politics was meteoric. By the time he was thirty years old, he had directed Len Jordan's successful 1950 gubernatorial campaign, been elected chairman of the Idaho Republican Party, and chaired Dwight D. Eisenhower's Idaho presidential campaign.

Campbell was born in Boise on March 10, 1922. He served as an infantry officer in World War II. After he graduated from the University of Idaho in 1949, he returned to Boise and opened an insurance agency. By the time he sold it in 1982, it was Idaho's largest independent insurance agency.

It was as the manager of Len Jordan's run for governor that Campbell cemented his reputation as one of Idaho's finest political strategists. Jordan was a rancher and car dealer from Grangeville. He was elected to the Idaho Legislature in 1946 and defeated in the next election. In 1950, Campbell determined that Jordan was a viable gubernatorial candidate, even with only a single legislative term behind him. Jordan won the election with 52 percent of the vote. Two years later, when Campbell chaired Eisenhower's Idaho campaign, he orchestrated a rally at the state capital that drew an estimated 19,000 people – still a record for the largest political rally ever held at the Statehouse.

When Campbell took over as Idaho Republican chairman in 1951, following Jordan's election, the Republicans held 29 seats in the State Senate and 36 seats in the House. In the 1952 election, thanks in large part of Campbell's organizational skills, they picked up four Senate seats and nine House seats.

Campbell managed more than fifty political campaigns in a period spanning nearly fifty years. He was active in Richard Nixon's campaigns and would later advise Idaho governors Phil Batt and Dirk Kempthorne. At the time of his death, the Associated Press stated that his political career was noted for "sound and well-thought-out policy, considerate action and great integrity."

Although he was an active University of Idaho alumnus who chaired the university's Alumni Association, he was also a founder of BSU's Bronco Athletic Association. In fact, next to politics, his greatest passion was sports and, especially, baseball. He was widely known as Boise's "Mr. Baseball."

Campbell devoted tireless hours to organizing and promoting youth baseball programs, such as American Legion baseball. He took an active role in Boise's professional baseball programs, serving as president of the Boise Braves from 1958-1962. Demonstrating his incredible promotional skills, Campbell convinced the Pittsburgh Pirates to come to Boise to play an exhibition game with the Braves in 1958. It was the largest crowd ever to gather for a baseball game in Boise, with an overflow crowd of 6,207 coming to see Meridian native Vernon Law pitch for the Pirates. In 1962, Campbell did a repeat, bringing the Milwaukee Braves to Boise to take on the Boise Braves.

After professional baseball went into a slump in Boise and the city found itself without a team for a number of years, it was Campbell who helped launch the successful formation of the Boise Hawks. In addition, he helped bring the Steelheads, a professional hockey team, to Boise.

When Campbell died in 2001, Boise's Cathedral of the Rockies was filled to capacity. As he was known to say at political events he organized, "Good crowd. Good crowd." At the conclusion of the service, everyone stood and sang "Take Me Out to the Ballgame."

63 David BALLARD

February 21, 1824 – September 18, 1883. Physician. Territorial governor. Buried: Lebanon, Oregon, Pioneer Cemetery.

The first two territorial governors of Idaho would seem obvious choices for this list. They do not make the cut. David Ballard, the third, was far more important to Idaho than either because he actually did the job he was supposed to do, the work of establishing the new territory as a governing unit.

To be sure, when the first territorial governor, William Wallace, arrived in Lewiston (then the capital) in 1863, he faced a terribly difficult task. An appointee of Abraham Lincoln, he was a representative of the hated federal government, a Republican appointee in an almost violently Democratic territory. Wallace's basic response was understandable, if unheroic: He contrived and conspired (and those would be accurate verbs) to get himself elected as territorial delegate to Congress, and made his escape from the territory as fast as possible. He did little useful by way of setting up a territorial government, or anything else; Idaho remained anarchic.

Of Wallace's successor, the pompous embezzler Caleb Lyon, suffice it here that one of the few positive things you could say about his tenure was that he made Wallace look good. As Ronald Limbaugh said soberly in his history *Rocky Mountain Carpetbaggers*: "The third governor of Idaho took office at the nadir of the territory's administrative history."

David Ballard was a physician who practiced medicine alongside his gubernatorial duties. He took what had been almost pure chaos and, with no meaningful help from Washington or anywhere else, gave Idaho Territory a solid, reasonably efficient, functional, and effective government. He brought governed civilization where two predecessors had failed completely.

How bad was it? No territorial bills had been paid in almost two years, and no sources of money were readily available. Conflicts among the new settlers and with the Native American tribes in the area were ongoing. Idaho's Democratic territorial delegate spent most of his time in Washington conniving to replace Ballard. And this delegate, Edward Holbrook, was so ferocious with his enemies that shortly after leaving Congress, he died of gunshot wounds in a shootout in downtown Idaho City.

Ballard, an appointee of Andrew Johnson (his appointment by a Democratic president may have helped him locally), put the indebted territory into the black for the first time. He established a stable government that formed the basis for later governments and, helped bring relative peace to the area. He also promoted and is largely responsible for the initial settlements in what is now the Fort Hall bottom lands, which provided one of the bases for later settlement in Eastern Idaho. The structure of government that has prevailed in Idaho state government for a century and a half was initially establish, in embryonic form, under Ballard.

A number of Idahoans actually asked the next president, Ulysses Grant, to keep Ballard in place, but Grant's appointment for territorial governor already had been made, and Ballard left office in March 1870. His departure was premature: Grant's appointee never showed up. Neither did the next one. And neither did the one after that. Idaho went for a couple of years before another presidentially-appointed governor actually appeared in Boise and took office. But Ballard's restructuring of territorial government, remarkably, mostly held.

Ballard, who had lived in Oregon before his Idaho appointment, returned there and died in 1883.

64 John HAILEY

August 29, 1835 – April 10, 1921. Ranching, mining. Delegate to Congress. Buried: Boise, Pioneer Cemetery.

John Hailey was a mayor of Boise, president of the Territorial Council in 1880, and a territorial delegate from Idaho to Congress. None of these runs in office was especially distinguished. His tenure as mayor was so brief that even its existence has been debated by historians (he was appointed in 1871 but apparently never took office). But Hailey was a busy man, and several of his other lines of work wound up leaving real imprints in Idaho.

A native of Tennessee, Hailey moved in the 1850s to Oregon, where he farmed and served in military battles. In 1862 he moved to Idaho, joining in the Boise Basin gold rush. Like many others, he found little gold but worked out other ways to make a living. In 1866 he bought the primitive (and even speculative) stage line running from Boise to The Dalles—no stage went all the way into the Willamette Valley then—and three years later the line running from near Salt Lake to Boise, giving him effective control of the lines through and out of southern Idaho. For a while he had the mail contract for the region, but lost it in 1870, and after that lost control of the stage line. He didn't give up. Shortly after his term in the U.S. House (1872-74), he formed new partnerships that regained control, under the name of the Utah, Idaho and Oregon Stage Company, of stages running from Boise east to Utah, south to Nevada, west to The Dalles and north to Walla Walla.

During these periods, shortly before rail would arrive, Hailey's decisions on stage routes would go on to influence later highway routes, and later settlement and development. Silver and lead were found in the Wood River Valley and sparked a rush in 1879, but the mines would begin to play out within a few years, and that valley could easily have gone the way of the Florence or Owyhee Mountain mines. Instead, Hailey ran a stage line in 1881 north into the Wood River Valley, and bought 440 riverside acres, setting them up as a townsite; he even moved there for a while to help guide development of the area. That site soon became the city of Hailey, forming the founding base for the Wood River Valley communities of Bellevue, Hailey, and Ketchum. Those developments might not have happened but for Hailey's routing decision and speculative land investment.

In 1899 he was named warden of the Idaho penitentiary, and helped set its path for decades to come. Perhaps more significant, in 1907 he was named the first Secretary and Librarian of the Idaho State Historical Society, giving him a key role in the organization of that agency. He took these responsibilities quite seriously, enough that he proceeded to write one of the first histories of Idaho in the years after.

65 Verda BARNES

February 23, 1907 – June 9, 1980. Chief of staff. Boise. Buried: Parker, cemetery.

Looking back to Idaho's not-too-distant political past, people ask how Democrats like Frank Church and Cecil Andrus could have gotten elected in such an overwhelmingly conservative Republican state. To a great extent, the answer is Verda Barnes.

President Franklin Roosevelt once told her that a good staff person "should have a passion for anonymity." She took his comment so much to heart that, except for Idaho political insiders active in the Church and Andrus eras, few have heard of her. But her impact on Idaho was substantial.

Verda White was born on February 23, 1907, in Willard, Utah. Shortly after that her family moved to a farm near St. Anthony, Idaho. After graduating from high school, she attended Albion Normal School and then transferred to Brigham Young University, graduating in 1930. She spent much of the 1930s in Boise where, after the repeal of prohibition, she was appointed by Governor C. Ben Ross to be the first director of operations for the Idaho Liquor Commission. The assumption being that by hiring a woman from a well-placed Mormon family, she would be above reproach.

Sometime in the 1930s she received a form letter from Jim Farley, the chairman of the Democratic National Committee, urging her to become involved in Roosevelt's New Deal. She got involved. She moved to Washington, D.C., first working as a political organizer for labor groups such as the CIO and the Amalgamated Clothing Workers, then working for the federal government. She became national vice-chairman of the Young Democrats and held positions with the Department of Interior, where she was an assistant to Secretary Harold Ickes, and the Securities and Exchange Commission, where she worked with William O. Douglas. She also established a close friendship with Eleanor Roosevelt.

Returning to her Idaho roots in 1945, she went to work for newly elected U.S. Senator Glen Taylor. After Taylor's defeat in 1950, she joined the staff of Congressman Pete Williams from New Jersey. When Frank Church was elected to the U.S. Senate in 1956, she moved to his staff, first as government liaison representative and eventually as his administrative assistant – chief of staff.

In that position she became chief political strategist for not only Church but for the entire Idaho Democratic Party.

Barnes was tireless. She spent her days working the phone, and plugging in to key operatives throughout Idaho and Washington, D.C. Republicans said that in a tight race, Barnes' arrival in Idaho always meant an additional 10,000 Democratic votes that otherwise wouldn't have been cast. Even when in Washington, she generally knew more about what was going on in Idaho than anyone on the ground in the state. She laid the groundwork for Church's successful re-election campaigns. She retired in 1975 and died months before the 1980 election, which Church lost by about 4,000 votes.

But perhaps her most lasting impact was in the rise of Cecil Andrus in statewide politics.

Andrus lost the 1966 primary election to Charles Herndon, but after Herndon was killed in a plane crash, Barnes began working the phones and eventually Andrus won the nomination from the State Democratic Central Committee by a single vote. Although he lost the 1966 election, four years later Barnes was back in the trenches. Using the statewide voter identification program she had put together for Church in 1968, along with much of his campaign volunteer base, plus the recruitment of several Church staff members working in a "boiler room" effort, she played a pivotal role in Andrus' election success in 1970, opening the door to one of the most successful political careers in Idaho history.

Barnes suffered a stroke and died on June 9, 1980. She is buried in the Parker cemetery near St. Anthony. Bill Hall, then editorial page editor for the *Lewiston Morning Tribune*, noted in an editorial: "They say that Verda Barnes died in her sleep the other night. But that's preposterous. Verda Barnes never slept."

66 Ernie DAY/ Bruce BOWLER

Bruce Bowler: March 24, 1911- May 2, 2002 Environmentalist, Attorney.

Ernie Day: 1918 – February 12, 2008 Environmentalist, Real Estate Developer.

Ernie Day snapped what probably is the single most significant photograph ever taken in Idaho. His shot of Castle Peak in the White Cloud Mountains set the stage for the most defining issue of the 1970 Idaho gubernatorial election: Should government allow an open pit mine there? Incumbent Don Samuelson said, "Yes!" Challenger Cecil Andrus said, "No!" Andrus unseated Samuelson and the White Clouds eventually became part of the 756,000-acre Sawtooth National Recreation Area.

Bowler helped put on the ballot the 1938 initiative creating the Department of Fish and Game. He also was instrumental in writing Idaho anti-dredge laws. In 1960, as counsel for the Idaho Wildlife Federation, he led the way in successfully challenging construction of both the Nez Perce and High Mountain Sheep dams on the Snake River.

But it is nearly impossible to separate Day's contributions from Bowler's. The two forged a partnership that has benefited and will continue to benefit generations of Idahoans and Idaho visitors.

Day and Bowler worked with Senator Frank Church on the development of both the Wilderness Act and the Wild and Scenic Rivers Act. It helped, of course, that Bowler had been Church's law partner in the latter's pre-Senate days. With Church playing pivotal roles in the Senate from 1957-1981 and Cecil Andrus as either governor or Secretary of the Interior during much of the period from 1971-1995, Day and Bowler were well positioned to have great influence on natural resource issues.

Bowler and Day teamed up in supporting the creation of the Hells Canyon National Recreation Area in 1975. Along with Ted Trueblood, they headed the River of No Return Wilderness Council. From that effort came the 2.367-million-acre River of No Return Wilderness, which is second only to Death Valley in size of a protected wilderness in the continental U.S. Near the end of Frank Church's life, his name would be added to the wilderness area.

Bruce Bowler was born in Shoshone, on March 24, 1911. He received his law degree from the University of Idaho in 1938 and immediately opened a Boise law practice, and began working as a volunteer for various environmental efforts. He practiced law for over fifty years and focused on both general law and environmental law. He died on May 2, 2002.

Ernie Day grew up in Boise. He graduated from the University of Idaho with a degree in political science and joined his family's real estate firm, Day Realty. With his father he developed Vista Village in Boise, Idaho's first shopping mall, and Ernie Day spent much of his adult life managing it. He was an avid backpacker and became concerned when he saw road accesses built into many of the places he enjoyed visiting. As a result, he became active in the environmental movement, serving on the board of the National Wildlife Federation, as president of the Idaho Wildlife Federation, and as chairman of the Idaho Parks Board. His outdoor photography won him the Ansel Adams photographic award.

During the decades Ernie Day and Bruce Bowler were active in Idaho's environmental movement, there were many other activists who played productive roles, but none as sweeping as Day and Bowler. When people look back and wonder who had the foresight to keep so much of Idaho's natural landscape from being developed, their names should be among the first to come to mind.

67 James L. "Doc" TAYLOR

? - November 15, 1982. Educator. Twin Falls.

Eugene Chaffee was by a long shot the single most influential figure in the history of Boise State University: He took a tiny private college in Boise, built it into a large and diverse institution, and took it to the brink of university status, though he didn't quite cross over into the promised land himself.

James L. "Doc" Taylor, of the College of Southern Idaho at Twin Falls, birthed his institution whole. It was nonexistent when he became its president. Through incredible drive and peerless political instincts, he left it a large, full-scale community college by the time he retired.

And he did it, year after year, keeping people amused.

A funny storyteller and a naturally gifted comedian, he provided his own sideshow as he won support from the Idaho Legislature, while undertaking what may have been the most remarkable empire-building operation in the history of Idaho government—certainly in Idaho higher education. Taylor was the paramount figure at the college during its first seventeen years and it was through his determination and skills that the college grew to become perhaps everything that a community college should be.

The institution's roots reach to October 1962, when civic leaders in Buhl supported the formation of the Idaho Technical Institute. They hired as its dean James L. Taylor, who had the advantage of secondary and post-secondary experience along with a doctorate from the University of Oklahoma at Norman. When the ITI folded in 1962, a new college, Southern Idaho College, was incorporated, and Taylor was one of the incorporators. He was also selected as president of the new college. The State Board of Education refused to allow the college to become a tax-supported institution due to a lack of a sufficient tax base. However, they did encourage establishment of a junior college in the Magic Valley.

With the demise of the Idaho Technical Institute and Southern Idaho College, Taylor left the area and became dean of men at Ellendale Teacher's College in North Dakota. Meantime, in November 1964, Twin Falls County citizens voted to form a junior college district and established the College of Southern Idaho. Taylor had impressed many during his stay in Buhl and, as a result, the CSI board of trustees voted unanimously to offer him the post of president. Taylor accepted and set about building a college from the ground up.

On September 1, 1965, the first 29 faculty had been hired and academic classes were held at Twin Falls High School, with most vocational classes taught at a rented building. Taylor and his board began looking for a permanent location for the campus and approval of a bond issue to begin construction. Once the site was selected, they succeeded in passing a $3 million bond issue, at the time the largest ever passed for education in Idaho. By 1968, the Fine Arts Center, the Shields Academy Building, a maintenance building, roads, parking, and utility work were underway. Months later work began on a dormitory and a physical education building. Next Taylor obtained state funding for a vocational-technical building.

One of the major challenges in establishing a new college is in obtaining accreditation. Taylor had focused much of his effort on recruitment of quality faculty, and that paid off when CSI was accredited in 1966.

Taylor was also both persuasive and innovative on meeting the funding needs for CSI. He convinced the Legislature to begin providing support from the state's Permanent Building Fund for community-college construction. To gain better operating efficiency as utility costs increased, he turned to geothermal heat. And, at a time when property taxes were the most unpopular tax in Idaho, he made the case for increased property tax support for CSI.

Doc Taylor was, by most measures, an authoritarian administrator. But he was also an astute lobbyist, whether going after additional federal funds or seeking support from the governor and legislature. He would appear before the legislature's Joint Finance-Appropriations Committee, take off his felt cowboy hat and rumpled raincoat, and walk to the podium with his leather briefcase. Speaking with no formal script, he would inevitably leave the committee asking if what he was requesting was all that he needed.

Taylor died November 15, 1982, and left a mature and thriving college where there had been nothing but farm fields.

68 Myran SCHLECHTE

March 22, 1930 – Currently lives in Parker, Colorado. Director, Idaho Legislative Council.

This listing of Idaho's 100 most influential citizens contains only a single person whose accomplishments are based solely upon his legislative activities: Myran Schlechte. He was not a legislator, and he never held any elective office. He was the first full-time professional staff person employed by the Idaho Legislature.

But also much more.

Schlechte served as director of the Idaho Legislative Council from 1963 until his retirement in 1991. For nearly three decades, he had more influence over Idaho's legislative process than any other single individual, legislative leaders included.

He was born in rural southeastern Nebraska on March 22, 1930 and grew up on a wheat ranch in Otis, Colorado. Following service in the Army during the Korean War, he enrolled at the University of Colorado and received an undergraduate degree in political science followed by a master's degree in public administration. In 1963, while serving on the staff of the Colorado Legislative Council, he applied for the newly created position of director of the Idaho Legislative Council.

During his 28 years working for the Idaho Legislature, he was at the forefront of developing much of the major legislation that now governs Idaho state government and the citizens of Idaho. The work of the Legislative Council included conducting studies, carrying out research, and drafting legislation. Among the more significant subjects Schlechte faced were court modernization, an updated Idaho municipal code, a revised Idaho constitution (which voters rejected), a revised criminal code, the Uniform Commercial Code, legislative reapportionment, the state sales tax, and a new probate code.

Schlechte had the good timing of coming to work for the legislature when perhaps the state's most effective and productive group of legislators was serving. The list includes, but only starts, with names like Pete Cenarrusa, Orval Hanesen, Charles McDevitt, James McClure, Darrell Manning, Cecil Andrus, and Phil Batt.

Under the leadership of these and other legislators, Schlechte established himself as the go-to person to discuss virtually any kind of legislative idea. He wasn't shy about providing counsel. He could make a good piece of legislation better through his research and drafting abilities. Quite often he would simply ignore a poorly thought-out piece of legislation and it would eventually die within the legislative process. In response to someone presenting such proposed legislation, he was known to crumple the paper on which it was written and dramatically throw it in the waste basket. His skills were so widely respected that he could get away with it.

When Schlechte was hired by the legislature in 1963, it met every two years, had a budget of $420,000 for legislative operations and another $50,000 for the Legislative Council, and occupied two floors of the state capitol. There was no full-time professional staff. When he retired in 1991, the Legislature had 57 full time staff, an annual budget of $7.3 million, and was meeting annually. Twenty years later, it had 72 full time legislative staff members, the annual budget had grown to $12.1 million, and the Legislature occupied four floors of the Statehouse, and beyond.

When Schlechte ran the Idaho Legislative Council, one of the posters on his office wall read: "Never teach a pig to sing. It wastes your time and it annoys the pig." That poster was a masterstroke of irony, because Schlechte spent most of his career (metaphorically) teaching pigs to sing, sometimes succeeding, and at least reducing the volume when he didn't. In the course of that, over a period of decades, he shaped the course of Idaho law and lawmaking more than any single Idaho legislator ever has or perhaps ever will.

69 William E. BORAH

June 29, 1865 – January 19, 1940. Attorney. U.S. Senator. Boise. Buried: Boise, Morris Hill Cemetery.

Possibly no Idahoan has had more widespread and long-lasting fame in his day than William E. Borah, senator from Idaho for 33 years. He's moderately well known even now, long after his death in 1940, and even in Idaho, where the state's highest mountain peak is named for him. Considering his long and influential history in the Senate, and his visible role in the formative days of Idaho around the turn of the century, the puzzle for some readers might be Borah's modest position on this list.

Simply put, Borah was a lot more influential in Washington than he was in Idaho. His impacts in Idaho concern mainly secondary echo-chamber effects and a handful of odds and ends. Once he left Idaho for Washington in 1907, he was truly at a remove. He was, for at least three decades, in the middle of the most important national and (especially) international issues facing the country, and he was one of the true lions of the Senate. He might rank higher than this on a list of the most influential senators of the twentieth century.

But: He kept just enough watch on Idaho politics to make sure his re-election wasn't at risk. It was a limited watch, since his popularity almost always ran high. Today's members of Congress can virtually commute between Washington, D.C. and their home state, but Borah (like many of his counterparts) returned to Idaho, ordinarily, only once every two or three years. An oft-repeated story, which may or may not be true, had a young Boise resident rushing home and telling his father that he had seen Senator Borah downtown. His father upbraided him for lying: "What would Senator Borah be doing in Boise?"

Once in the Senate he played little role in internal state politics, and hardly any in the state Republican Party, which was run throughout his Senate tenure by political opponents who were much more stereotypically conservative than Borah was. He kept himself aloof and apart. When in 1936 he was challenged by a popular Democratic governor, C. Ben Ross, Borah was asked what he had done specifically for the state; his response was an embarrassingly skimpy list. So great was his reputation, and so senator-like was he, that he won in another landslide anyway, in a big Democratic year. Yet, unlike some other relatively important figures Idaho has sent to Washington, Borah left little behind to note his presence in his home state.

He makes the list for several scattered reasons.

First, his mere presence in the Senate for so long had some reverberating impact. It irritated but reined in some of the more conservative Republicans of his time. It provided some encouragement, actually, for Democrats. He was an inspiration to quite a few, including Frank Church, who saw Borah as a hero to emulate (and did, in his lengthy Senate tenure, chairmanship of the Foreign Relations Committee, and unsuccessful run for president).

Second, his activities in the turn-of-the-century Idaho GOP gave it a distinctively conservative rather than populist spin. His election to the Senate took him out of Idaho politics, and thereby deprived Idaho of its main Bull Moose progressive voice. His absence helped conservatives to flourish.

And his work as an attorney had important side effects for Boise and Idaho. He was one of the earliest really skillful attorneys in Idaho, and played an important role in the Haywood murder conspiracy trial and other cases of note. He also had a small role in irrigation development (helping one developer almost complete a line to Boise, an effort later completed).

But, in all, less of an impact on Idaho than you might think.

70 | C.C. Van ARSDOL

August 19, 1851 - February 25, 1941. Engineer. Lewiston. Buried: Lewiston, Normal Hill Cemetery.

Cassius Cash Van Arsdol, better known as C.C., was born near Muncie, Indiana, on August 19, 1851. He graduated in the first engineering class at the University of Iowa in 1876 with a degree in civil engineering. After graduation he became a surveyor for railroad routes; first for the St. Louis, Kansas City and Northern Railroad and then, in 1880, for the Union Pacific in Omaha. In 1887 he became Pacific Northwest Division Engineer for Union Pacific.

In the early 1880s, Lewiston businessman Alonzo Leland had traveled to Omaha to try to persuade the Union Pacific to build a rail line from Lewiston up the Clearwater River. Now, five years later, Van Arsdol accepted Leland's invitation and visited Lewiston for the first time. It was the beginning of Van Arsdol's relationship with North Central Idaho, a connection in which he, perhaps more than any other individual, made possible the continuing commercial development of that region.

It is probably safe to say that anyone who has traveled in the area between McCall and Moscow has been able to do so because of Van Arsdol's engineering efforts. His work covered some of the most difficult geographic terrain imaginable.

Van Arsdol's initial work was in surveying railroad routes. He surveyed the route from Lewiston to Kamiah and downstream on the Snake River to Riperia. He also surveyed the rail route from Mullan, Idaho, to Missoula, Montana, which closely parallels today's Interstate 90. He surveyed two other rail routes that were never constructed: Weiser to Lewiston following the Snake River through Hells Canyon, and Orofino to Missoula, which was the precursor to U.S. 12. He also attempted to survey a route through the Salmon River Canyon, but was forced to give up on it.

With the advent of motor vehicles, he turned his engineering efforts to highways. The most prominent was the Lewiston Spiral Highway, which connected Lewiston with Spokane and other points north. In addition, he engineered both the original Whitebird Grade and the Winchester Grade. His Pomeroy Grade opened up a highway route leading from Idaho to Walla Walla and ultimately to Portland. Similarly, his grade into and out of the Grand Ronde River canyon opened the way from the Lewiston area south into Enterprise and eastern Oregon.

In addition, two of his early railroad surveys, the Mullen to Missoula route and the Orofino to Missoula route, would eventually become the routes of major highways.

In 1911, a banquet was held in his honor in Lewiston. The main speaker was Henry Adams, the grandson of John Quincy Adams and author of the widely read autobiography *"The Education of Henry Adams."* Henry's brother, Charles Francis Adams, Jr., was president of Union Pacific from 1884-1890.

Van Arsdol was nearly ninety years old when he died on February 25, 1941.

Perhaps his life was best summed up by the *Lewiston Morning Tribune*: "By profession, Mr. Van Arsdol was a civil engineer. In instinct, he was a practical dreamer." He is buried in Normal Hill Cemetery in Lewiston. A monument near the top of the old Lewiston Spiral Highway commemorates his life and accomplishments.

71 John TOURTELLOTTE/ Charles F. HUMMEL

Tourtellotte: February 22, 1869 – 1939. Architect. Boise.
Hummel: April 2, 1857 - 1939. Architect. Boise.

John Tourtellotte and Charles F. Hummel were the designers of many of Idaho's most readily recognizable buildings. Their work took them to every corner of the state, and today their projects stand as some of Idaho's finest and most historic buildings and homes.

Tourtellotte was born in East Thompson, Connecticut, in 1869. At 17, he became an apprentice in an architectural firm in Webster, Massachusetts. He then migrated west, working on various construction projects until he arrived in Boise in 1890. There he founded a firm that was involved in both construction and architecture, eventually focusing solely on architecture.

Hummel was born in Germany and classically trained as an architect and engineer. After stops in Chicago and Seattle, he arrived in Boise in 1895. He joined Tourtellotte's firm as an architect, and later the two formed the partnership of Tourtellotte and Hummel.

They were a perfect match for what would become a thriving business; Hummel the classically trained architect who understood all of the engineering requirements of the structures they designed, and Tourtellotte, a superb designer and promoter.

Their most famous project was Idaho's capitol building. Others included: the Administration Building and Memorial Gymnasium at the University of Idaho; the Boise High School campus; Gooding College campus (later the Idaho TB Hospital); Boise's Elks Temple; the Knights of Pythias Castle in Weiser; the Boise Junior College administration building; Lewiston Vineyards gates; Nampa First Methodist Episcopal Church; St. Charles of the Valley Catholic Church in Hailey; Bruneau Episcopal Church; Owyhee County courthouse; St. John's Roman Catholic Cathedral in Boise; the Weiser Post Office; and the Washington County courthouse.

The list of projects they were involved in is so extensive that the National Register of Historic Places maintained by the Department of Interior lists 149 homes and buildings in Idaho that were designed by Tourtellotte and/or Hummel. It is a testament to their skills that so many of their buildings remain standing today.

In 1922, Tourtellotte moved to Portland and opened an office with Frank Hummel, Charles's son.

They designed a number of significant buildings in Oregon, too, including the Redwoods Hotel in Grants Pass. Tourtellotte retired in 1930 and died in 1939.

Charles Hummel remained in Boise and continued his architectural practice, which would eventually include three generations of the Hummel family. Hummel Architects continues as one of Idaho's leading architectural firms. Charles Hummel died in 1939.

72 Perry SWISHER

September 21, 1923 – June, 6, 2012. Journalist, Legislator, Public Utilities Commissioner. Boise/Pocatello.

Raised as a polio-stricken youngster on a remote ranch in Owyhee County, Perry Swisher became maybe the single most remarkable public personality Idaho has ever seen, unconstrained by almost any simplistic description.

Consider this from a profile by colleague Jay Shelledy (April 8, 1979) when Swisher departed a job at the *Lewiston Morning Tribune* to take a seat on the state Public Utilities Commission: "As a journalist, legislator, gardener, publisher, guru, crusader, advisor to the mighty and the molested, critic, bard, counselor wondrous, administrator, confessor, orator, pundit laureate and consummate pain in the posterior – to place the adjective 'former' in front of those titles is not to know the man – Perry Swisher has been handing down observations and decrees ever since he presided over his Owyhee County birth 55 years ago. On the surface, he can be outrageous. Until you roll those pronouncements around in your tattered brain a while. It is then you discover Perry Swisher uses shock value well."

In the '40s he was living in Pocatello (after attending college there), writing about the region and its politics for the *Salt Lake Tribune* and running for the legislature, and sometimes winning despite his status as a Republican in Democratic Bannock County. He ran several businesses, including a restaurant (the only one, he once said, that consistently made money), a bookstore, and a weekly newspaper, the *Intermountain*—which produced some of the best political writing and reading in Idaho. After an unsuccessful run for governor as an independent in 1966, a race undertaken to support the state's new sales tax, his paper was merged with a Boise weekly to become the *Intermountain Observer*, provider of much of the best journalism in the state for nearly a decade. Swisher worked for a time as an administrator at Idaho State University, then as night managing editor of the *Lewiston Morning Tribune*. Swisher was appointed by Gov. John Evans in 1979 to the Idaho Public Utilities Commission which he left in 1985. He continued writing columns well into the new millennium.

That description only scratches the surface. No one of Swisher's labors of love singly transformed Idaho (the sales tax possibly excepted), but together they added up.

He was one of several essential figures in the passage of Idaho's sales tax by the legislature in 1965 and by the electorate the next year. His entry in the 1966 race may have (Swisher himself argued against it) cost Cecil Andrus election as governor that year; but then, Andrus was four crucial years younger, and had far less unified Democratic Party support at that time than when he was elected in 1970; Andrus might not have been near the governor he became had he been "prematurely" elected.

Swisher was a key influence on the utilities commission, and probably changed the state's utilities policy in significant ways, not least the change in pay phone costs rising from a dime to a quarter.

Swisher presents a problem, one he might happily have pondered, on the matter of influence. Aside from his work on sales tax and utility issues, you can't draw many short or straight lines between Swisher and specific changes in law, policy, business, or politics. But the indications are there if you look for them. The fact that in order to serve on the Supreme Court you have to be an attorney, stems directly with a rumor that non-attorney Swisher was under consideration for appointment to the court. And numerous journalists sharpened their work both from listening to Swisher's counsel and out of fear that he would take them to task.

Few people thought about Idaho, where it was and where it was going, as deeply as he did, or communicated those often otherwise unheard of ideas so well, or reached, with such punch and power, the broad range of Idahoans who were making many things happen. An attorney might say that Swisher was not always a proximate cause, but that he was part of the nexus of what happened: Of many things that happened.

73 Alfred BUDGE

February 24, 1868 – January 25, 1951. Attorney. Supreme Court justice.

Probably it says something that Alfred Budge served longer on the Idaho Supreme Court than anyone ever has. A slice of the reason for his presence here is simply the volume of work he delivered between his appointment to the court in 1914 and his retirement in 1949. He is estimated to have written more than 1,000 court decisions, almost certainly more than any other Idaho Supreme Court justice. He served more than half a century in elective office.

But the most compelling argument for his inclusion here was not his work as a justice, or a judge, or even as Bear Lake County prosecutor. It was his status as a defendant in a lawsuit.

A native of Providence, Utah (he would be the first Idaho Supreme Court justice born in the West), Budge studied law and took his law degree in Michigan, and moved soon after to Bear Lake County. Well-connected – the Budges were prominent both in the local communities and in the LDS Church even then – he became county prosecutor in 1898.

Four years later, he was elected district judge, and therein lay the issue. His re-election to the post in 1906 drew a legal challenge on grounds that Budge was a practicing Mormon, and that Mormons were barred from holding state office. Unlike some of his brethren, Budge did not back off; he insisted, as it were, on his day in court. And an important day that was.

Over the preceding years, the stringent anti-Mormon provisions of the 1890 state constitution, which sought to bar members of the church from voting and from holding office, had been increasingly ignored, but they had not been repealed outright. (That would not happen until voters in 1978 approved a constitutional amendment to that effect.) Mormons were beginning to play a significant role in Idaho government and politics, but that role as yet existed in a gray area.

Toncray v. Budge, one of the most significant legal cases in Idaho history, took on the issue directly, and in it the Idaho Supreme Court decided squarely in Budge's favor. Idaho politics and culture changed significantly afterward.

More directly, it allowed Budge later to move up to the Supreme Court. But the impacts went far beyond Budge alone.

74 Phil REBERGER

1942 - . Chief of staff; campaign manager. Boise.

Phil Reberger is a classic example of an unseen power, a person who makes things happen while rarely surfacing to public view. (See also on this list, Verda Barnes.) On the few occasions he has, he wastes no time submerging again. But of his influence over the course of now more than three decades, there's no doubt.

His resume tells only part of the story. A Canyon County native, Reberger went to work in national Republican Party politics, and in the '70s was involved in several important Republican campaigns, including that of Virginia Senator John Warner. In 1978 he returned to Idaho to take on a relatively easy assignment, getting James McClure re-elected to the Senate. He impressed onlookers with his crisp professionalism: McClure's re-election was never in doubt, but the campaign was run uncommonly well. Reberger came across as an absolute pragmatist: he once told one of the authors that he cared only about getting McClure 50 percent plus one of the vote.

His next campaign, that of Steve Symms for the Senate in 1980, was far more difficult; without Reberger's skill at the helm, Symms might not have won that razor-close race. Reberger also helmed Symms through a tough re-election in 1986, and helped give Dirk Kempthorne a big win in 1992 in what at one point looked like a difficult challenge.

His work in keeping that Senate seat Republican is the start of it. Reberger also has been a key staffer for Symms and Kempthorne, and has cut a big figure in federal politics in Idaho. His campaign skill and his influence with other Republicans are considerable.

Reberger's real-world impact has been a lot greater than that of many people who have actually won elective office in Idaho. He probably would have the campaign skills to run and win an office, if he chose; but why take a step down?

In later years, he did serve and did significant work as a member of the Idaho Judicial Council, the Boise Airport Commission and for the Boise Redevelopment Agency,

Dial back to 1980, to the superhot politics of that year, when Ronald Reagan challenged Jimmy Carter for the presidency, and in Idaho a Senate seat was locked in a close battle between four-term incumbent Frank Church and Republican challenger Steve Symms.

History has a way of creating inevitabilities, waves that seem in hindsight to be massive historical trends, but for a long time 1980 looked like a close call. Carter was managing slim leads in many polls and stayed close not long before election day. And the Idaho Senate race was, for months and right up to election day, very close. Out of about 440,000 votes cast in that race, Symms won by 4,262, a sliver so slight that any of a dozen factors could have tipped it the other way. Put another way, Idaho politics might have taken a very different trajectory. With more Church years in the Senate, Democrats might have been in a much stronger position in Idaho, and the Republican climate much different. The line of steady Republican succession to the Senate and other major offices would have been disrupted; the partisan trajectory in the '90s might have been a lot different.

75 Andrew LITTLE

December 19, 1870 - February 20, 1941. Sheep rancher. Emmett. Buried: Emmett.

To say that Andy Little was a sheep rancher is a bit like saying that Henry Ford worked on cars. He was known as Idaho's Sheep King and was the owner of possibly the largest sheep operation in the entire nation.

Little, born in Moffatt, Scotland, on December 19, 1870, came to Idaho in 1893 with a bedroll and two sheep dogs. Getting off of the train in Caldwell, he walked 22 miles to the Robert Aikman Ranch near Emmett where he had been offered a job as a sheepherder. He purchased his first band of 1,200 sheep a year later and the following year acquired 40 acres of land.

Little began building his sheep empire and never looked back. At one time he owned 100,000 sheep and grazed them on lands that extended from Boise to the Salmon River. At the peak of his operations in 1929, he shipped an estimated one million pounds of wool. In 1936, in addition to wool, he also marketed 66,000 lambs. The exact size of his operations was never known, since he didn't feel that it was appropriate to talk about it. But he did own 27 separate irrigated ranches that were used to raise all of the hay and grain he needed to feed his sheep during the winter months. His sheep bands were also broken up into smaller units and at one time he employed an estimated 400 people.

Little also enjoyed a national reputation as one of the major stockmen in the country. His portrait hangs in the Saddle and Sirloin Club in Louisville, Kentucky, along with those of other major leaders in the nation's livestock industry over the twentieth century. As the Club defines its portrait gallery, "It is a portrayal of how men's minds and hearts along with courage and hard work can achieve and benefit society."

Although he was not particularly active in politics, his family became one of the best-known political families in Idaho. His son Dave served one term in the Idaho House and five terms in the Idaho Senate. His nephew Walt served ten terms in the Idaho House and was majority leader there, and his grandson Brad was elected to four terms in the Idaho Senate and in 2009 became Idaho's 37th lieutenant governor.

Andy Little died on February 20, 1941. A news article said that he was "broad-gauged, very systematic and humane. Much of his strength lay in his ability to handle labor. He was exacting in his methods, kept his men busy 12 months out of the year, and, after they became familiar with it, they liked his methods. Many men now in the outfits have served faithfully for more than 20 years...."

76 John V. EVANS

January 18, 1925 - . Banker. Governor. Malad, Burley.

John Evans' political career would be remarkable if for no other reason than that in one of the most Republican states in the nation, he served – as a Democrat – as Senate majority leader, Senate minority leader, lieutenant governor and governor. He also served as mayor of Malad, a city in heavily Republican southeastern Idaho.

Evans was born into a political family, in Malad, on January 18, 1925. His grandfather, David L. Evans, served in the territorial legislature and was also an early Speaker of the House after statehood. His father was Oneida County Democratic Party chairman. John Evans was first elected to the state Senate at 27, in the Republican year of 1952.

Elected lieutenant governor in 1974, Evans moved up to governor in 1977 when Governor Cecil Andrus resigned to become secretary of the Interior. He shortly found himself in the midst of a perfect storm. A drought was causing severe hardship on the state. And in 1978 Idaho voters approved a one-percent property tax limitation, forcing public schools and local governments to become even more reliant on the state than they had previously been. At the same time Idaho's economy began a decline, due in large part to low prices for agricultural commodities, timber, and minerals. By 1980 the state was in the midst of its greatest economic crisis since the Great Depression.

Many governors would not have survived long in office under those conditions. Evans' popularity actually rose, however, and he followed his two years as a governor by succession with election to two full terms.

In the early '80s the Swan Falls water rights issue, with the potential of removing irrigation water from hundreds of thousands of acres of farm land, landed on his desk. Evans worked with Idaho Power, the Legislature, Attorney General Jim Jones, and the agricultural community to reserve future water rights for development upstream from Swan Falls. This also led to the largest water rights adjudication effort in the nation's history.

The economic downturn and the resulting budget problems most strongly put Evans' wide range of skills to the test. He often was at odds with the early '80s Republican legislative leadership, House Speaker Tom Stivers and Senate President pro tem Jim Risch, but even so enacted much of his agenda working with coalitions of Democrats and moderate Republicans. (He also used, and became known for, his big red veto stamp.) That agenda included selected spending cuts and a wide range of tax increases. And, while state agencies were hit with a series of budget holdbacks and state workers were reduced to 32-hour work weeks, public schools were largely held harmless. In addition, he established the Department of Commerce, with a focal point of its activity the increase of the state's tourism. Using a two-percent hotel-motel room tax, the state was able to expand its tourism promotion program and make tourism the third largest segment of the state's economy.

Evans' track record of success in dealing with Republican legislatures was, in many instances, better than those of his Republican successors.

In 1986, he unsuccessfully ran for the U.S. Senate against incumbent senator Steve Symms. It was his only loss in a 34-year span in which his name appeared on the ballot 23 times.

After leaving the governorship, Evans moved to Burley to take over the family banking business. From that point, D.L. Evans Bank expanded rapidly from its base in Burley and Malad to spread across southern Idaho, including seven locations in Boise.

77 Charles F. McDEVITT

January 5, 1932 – Pocatello. Attorney, corporate executive, legislator, judge. Boise.

Few people can claim to have had major public influence spanning half a century, but such is the case with Charles McDevitt. Over those 50 years he served as a member of the Idaho legislature, as a corporate executive, chief justice of the Idaho Supreme Court, a public defender, and a community volunteer. Most people would consider service on the Idaho Supreme Court to be a career high watermark, but McDevitt's actually may have come years earlier, in 1965.

Born in Pocatello in 1932, McDevitt entered law school at the University of Idaho when he was twenty years old. After one year of law school, he volunteered for a two-year stint in the Army. While he was under orders to go to Korea, his law school experience came to the attention of Army officials and he was asked to form and head up a special unit to focus on handling cases of deserters and AWOL soldiers. Following his discharge from the Army, he re-entered law school and graduated in 1956.

In 1962 he was elected to the Idaho legislature from Ada County. In the 1963 session, concerned about school funding and the state's tax structure, he sponsored legislation to establish a state sales tax. The bill passed the House, but failed in the Senate. In 1963 he ran for national chair of the Young Republicans, and lost by three votes. In 1965, as vice-chairman of the House Revenue and Taxation Committee, he again sponsored sales tax legislation. This time his bill passed both House and Senate and, as a statewide referendum, was approved by the voters. Having accomplished his goal of establishing a sales tax, he chose not to run for re-election.

In 1962 he left his private law practice and went to work for Boise Cascade, where he served as general counsel, secretary, and vice president. He was also a founder and member of the board of directors of Farmers and Merchants State Bank. In 1968 he became president of Beck Industries in New York City and then executive vice president of the Singer Corporation. He moved back to Boise in 1976 and, following service as the Ada County public defender, formed the law firm of Givens, Pursley, McDevitt and Webb, which went on to become one of Idaho's largest.

In 1989, Governor Cecil Andrus appointed McDevitt to the Idaho Supreme Court. In 1993 he became chief justice. There he used his corporate executive skills to completely rework the internal administrative structure of the court. Among cases he played a role in during his tenure on the court was determining how the massive Snake River Basin water adjudication would work.

After retiring from the court in 1997, he returned to private practice and began to focus much of his spare time on expanding recreational opportunities for southwest Idaho citizens. His philosophy was that keeping young people busy with work and play keeps them out of trouble. His first effort was to expand youth soccer in Boise, which had no soccer facilities. He took the lead in developing a 160-acre soccer complex in southeast Boise that would have twenty soccer fields and nine softball fields, plus an extensive trail system. He also led development of a local soccer tournament and eventually turned it into a seven state tournament, and worked on developing a thirteen-acre soccer complex in Nampa.

In 2001, as chair of the city of Boise's Foothills Conservation Advisory Committee, he led a successful campaign for a $10 million serial levy to assist in preserving land in the Boise foothills from future development. has helped to preserve over 10,000 acres in the Boise foothills, which now contains between 80-90 miles of hiking trails. McDevitt has also served on the boards of both the Girl Scouts and the Boise YMCA. In recognition of his wide-ranging support of youth activities, the city of Boise named a forty-acre youth sports complex in West Boise the Charles F. McDevitt Sports Complex. It features several little league fields, a picnic area, a playground, a skate park, and fishing pond.

78 Aaron PARKER

March 16, 1856 - January 4, 1930. Newspaper publisher.

By the time Aaron Parker was 21 years old, he had spent five years at sea, prospected for gold in Idaho, and taken an active part in the Nez Perce Indian War. Before long, he would publish several newspapers around Idaho. The common thread was Parker's penchant for travel, especially in the Inland Northwest, and part of his lasting legacy in Idaho was the road – still the only one – directly connecting northern and southern Idaho.

Born in Wells, England, on March 16, 1856, Parker went to sea at age 12. At age 17 he arrived in Idaho to prospect for gold. In 1877, at age 21, he joined with General Oliver Howard during the Nez Perce War and became a messenger, carrying messages on horseback and on foot to Boise.

His brother Frank became publisher of a daily newspaper in Walla Walla, and soon Aaron followed him into the newspaper business. In 1883 he moved to Eagle City, Idaho, the first mining camp in the Coeur d'Alenes. (At about that same time, Wyatt Earp and his brothers arrived in Eagle City and opened a saloon called The White Elephant.) Parker then moved to Coeur d'Alene where he founded and published the *Coeur d'Alene Eagle*. Next, he moved to Lewiston, where he edited the *Nez Perce Journal* and, finally, to Grangeville, where he established the *Idaho County Free Press* (the only one of these papers still in publication) in 1886.

Parker had first visited the Camas Prairie as a prospector and recognized strong possibilities for economic growth in the area. He used his newspaper to spread the word that the area around

Grangeville held unlimited possibilities. In 1889, the citizens of Idaho County elected him to be their representative at Idaho's constitutional convention. At the convention, he played one of the two most significant roles he would play in Idaho.

Upon becoming a state, Idaho was to receive major tracts of federal land earmarked to benefit public schools. The general feeling among the delegates was that these lands could be sold with the proceeds providing immediate benefit to the new state. Parker disagreed. In a speech on the convention floor he said, "Let us hold on to them, and not sell them now at a minimum price to land grabbers and speculators, and deprive our children of their common heritage. Let us hold on to them, and as our territory develops these lands will increase in value and we shall be able to get money for school purposes without calling upon the people for direct taxation for money for educational purposes…"

He succeeded in building up support for his position among a majority of convention delegates and, while he wasn't correct about endowment earnings providing all of the funding needs for public schools, they would nevertheless eventually provide hundreds of millions of dollars for public schools.

After the convention, Parker took up another project that would also have major beneficial implications for much of the state. He became the primary promoter of a north-south wagon road. He was tireless, and by the time he died, at Spokane on January 4, 1930, the wagon road he had so strongly promoted had become the North-South Highway and was being used by cars and trucks. We know much of it now, in paved and much improved condition, as U.S. Highway 95.

79 Thomas HUMBIRD

1865 – 1954. Timber executive. Sandpoint.

Sandpoint, located in one of Idaho's most beautiful areas, was a late bloomer for human settlement. It was not especially obscure. It had become a small but periodic trading point as early as 1810. But no permanent settlers arrived until the mid-1880s, because there seemed to be no good reason.

Much of the land in the area was forested, hard to access for farming or for marketing produce, and beyond that the climate and soil weren't amenable to more than a narrow band of crops. The Silver Valley to the southeast had excited plenty of interest, but there seemed to be no good mining opportunities around Sandpoint (though some smaller mines eventually were developed to the east near Clark Fork). The few settlers in the Sandpoint area didn't form a village until 1900, and then because rail had begun to run through the area.

That marked, however, the opportunity Thomas Humbird had been looking for.

He was the son of John Humbird, who ran several mid-sized timber operations in Wisconsin, and was a partner in several deals with Northwest timber magnate Frederick Weyerhaeuser. With rail lines in place – the chicken-and-egg sequence here may be debatable – connecting Spokane with the area from Newport, Washington, through Priest River over to Sandpoint, the Humbirds and Weyerhaeuser decided to launch a string of timber operations. Sandpoint's, evidently the largest, was started in 1902, under Thomas Humbird's direct management. For decades it was a major timber center, one of the largest cedar pole producers and shippers in the western states.

That was the real founding of Sandpoint, and the creation as well of its long-running timber-town culture. In more recent years, as the mills closed, its economy has become more based around its retirees, arts communities, and other interests, but the hard-working timber culture remains.

Humbird remains little known, but a small-populated area, a street in Sandpoint and an election precinct are named for him.

80 George L. YOST

December 6, 1905 – October 21, 1995 Fruit grower, fruit cooperative executive.

Nearly every industry has at least one person who can be looked to as its leading activist. For the Idaho fruit industry, that person would be George Yost. During the years of the twentieth century when the fruit-growing industry was at its peak, he was involved in nearly every aspect of the industry and even co-authored a book, *Idaho, the Fruitful Land*, about the history of fruit growing in Idaho.

George Yost was born on December 6, 1905, in Guthrie, Indian Territory, now Oklahoma. The next year he moved to the Boise Valley with his parents, growing up near Ustick (just west of Boise) and graduating from the University of Idaho. He then returned home and worked for his father in his fruit brokerage business, assembling boxcar loads of various types of produce for shipment throughout the United States.

In 1933 he became manager of Gem Fruit Union, a growers cooperative based in Emmett, and also of Diamond Fruit Growers of Idaho, after Gem Fruit merged with Diamond. Using lessons he learned working for his father, he developed marketing and shipping plans that benefited many, if not most, fruit growers in southwestern Idaho. An example of the success of the Gem Fruit Union was annual shipments of prunes that reached as high as 325 rail cars of prunes alone. Yost also operated orchards of his own up until a few years before his death.

George Yost quickly became the go-to guy for Idaho's fruit industry. He served as president and secretary of the Idaho

Horticultural Society, president of the Idaho-Oregon Growers and Shippers Association, president of the Idaho Prune Commission, president of the Idaho Cooperative Council, president of the Gem Labor Council, chairman of the University of Idaho Agricultural Consulting Council, and a member of the Idaho Apple Commission and the Idaho Water Resources Board.

Yost was also very active in civic affairs. He served as mayor of Emmett, a member of the Emmett School Board, and president of the Emmett Chamber of Commerce. He also served as president of the University of Idaho Alumni Association and, in recognition of his professional work in the fruit industry, was awarded an honorary doctorate degree by the university.

In recent years, except for grape production, Idaho's fruit industry has been declining. Some of this has been because of increased operating costs, but much of it has also been due to the removal of orchards to make way for housing and other types of development. During much of the peak activity period for the industry, George Yost was its guiding force and his efforts had a major impact on Idaho's economy for many years. Yost died on October 21, 1995, at his home in Emmett.

81 Ron TWILEGAR

September 18, 1943 - . Attorney. State senator, city council member. Boise.

Attorney and businessman Ron Twilegar was a member of the Idaho Senate and the Boise city council, and had some impact on both places. Unusually for this list, though, he's here more for the politics surrounding those offices than for what he did in them.

Ron Jess Twilegar is a native of Vancouver, Washington, but has lived most of his life in Idaho – mainly in the Boise area, working as an attorney and developer of a string of innovative businesses. He has been a political entrepreneur as well, a seeker after opportunities few other people saw. Not all of them panned out, but at least two made a major difference.

In the early '70s, not only Ada County but Boise as well was solidly Republican. As 1974 dawned, Boise had not elected a Democrat to the legislature in decades – and voted solidly Republican in local and other state offices as well. But Twilegar, a young politician operating outside much of the state Democratic structure, saw changes in Boise – a growing state government with more government employees, and the rapid growth of what became Boise State University that year. He decided to run for the Idaho House in the district encompassing Boise's North End and he struck the right notes in his campaign. Twilegar defeated Republican Ferd Koch, a five-term House member then thought to have an inside track on becoming House speaker. Two years later, he went after the powerful chairman of the Senate State Affairs Committee, five-term senator H. Dean Summers. The North End of Boise was changing, and Twilegar was the political figure who leveraged that.

What he launched then has since become entrenched. The Senate seat he won in 1976 has stayed in Democratic hands, and for the last two decades the two House seats in that district likewise remained Democratic. That North End district became a sort of Democratic redoubt from which Democrats could reach out to win more seats in nearby Boise districts. In the new millennium they wound up winning a number of them.

In 1983, after leaving the legislature, Twilegar ran for and won a seat on the Boise city council. In winning that seat, he played a pivotal role in a moment of change at Boise. The city was enmeshed in a bitter debate over the future of its downtown and economic redevelopment. Twilegar planted himself solidly on the side opposing three-term Boise mayor Dick Eardley's plan, and was a central figure in leading the opposition. He did that on the council and behind the scenes, where he helped reshape the contours of the alliances that dominated city politics – helping create alliances of Republicans and Democrats and others who fit no category. The city decisively changed course after Eardley retired and was replaced by new mayor Dirk Kempthorne, a future governor and senator, whose arrival as mayor was due in considerable part to Twilegar's strategy. Twilegar departed the scene.

He remained visible and active, from 1983 – 1990 he chaired the Capitol City Development Corporation, Boise's downtown redevelopment agency, and running unsuccessfully for the U.S. Senate in 1990 against Republican Larry Craig. More recently he been active, sometimes controversially, in local government. But his work at two decisive moments in Boise political history account for his place in this list.

82 | John B. NEIL

1842 - October 6, 1902. Territorial office. Territorial governor. Boise. Buried: Columbus, Ohio, Green Lawn Cemetery.

John Neil was not governor of Idaho Territory for long, but he had as much impact as any on the territory—turning its partisan politics upside down, initiating a wave of religious persecution that lasted most of a couple of decades, and setting Idaho directly on the road to statehood.

It all grew out of one mainspring: He despised Mormons, as did President Rutherford B. Hayes, who in August 1880 promoted Neil from the land office at Salt Lake City. Hayes tasked Neil with a specific mission, which Neil got underway immediately: Clamp down on Mormons and thereby upend Idaho politics.

From the mining beginnings of Idaho politics, the territory had leaned Democratic (meaning, in its early days, pro-southern). Infusions of midwestern and northeastern farmers and timber workers gradually changed the equation, and by the time Neil was sworn in the Democrats' main asset keeping them in a majority was the also-growing Mormon vote, closely allied with the Democrats. Hayes had tried to disenfranchise Mormons with national legislation, but didn't succeed so he began a more localized attack. Arriving in Idaho, Neil made the end of polygamy (still a decade away from repudiation by the church), and the crushing of Mormons his top objective. A day after his swearing-in, he took charge of reapportionment to further his cause. He started speaking against "the Mormon menace" wherever he went. He appointed anti-Mormon radicals to key spots wherever he could. When Congress passed the Edmunds Act in early 1882, denying polygamists most rights of citizenship, Neil used that law to press further. He used the Mormon issue, as well, to bring northern Idaho secessionists into alliance with his Republicans, forming the first enduring Republican majority Idaho had seen – one that, with important shifts and moves, endures today.

Neil was removed from office in the spring of 1883 for reasons still unclear. Unlike most territorial governors, he stayed in the territory, retiring on a ranch in the Wood River Valley. By then his anti-Mormon campaign was slowing down. Internal Republican Party factions were providing obstacles. His immediate successor spent less than a month in Idaho, and the next governor after that was relatively uninterested in persecuting Mormons.

But by the time Neil's crusade was riding high, a new U.S. Marshal based at Blackfoot, Fred T. Dubois, had taken office and soon would take up the cause himself. That cause crashed and burned early in the next century, but along the way it left an important side effect: Idaho statehood.

83 William RODEN

1929 - . State senator. Attorney. Boise.

How to assess the influence of a lobbyist, who pursues not so much an individual, personal agenda, but rather that of an employer; and whose influence is filtered through that of the people he tries to influence? How to do it, moreover, when much of what that lobbyist does is far from visible, when his actions leave only subtle traces?

There's no perfect answer. Much of what Lloyd Adams and Tom Boise did came in their capacity as lobbyists, but they were something more besides: Influence brokers, true dealmakers, whose impact went beyond those people and interests they happened to represent.

In some ways, on a more limited scale, some of the same is true of Bill Roden, a Boise attorney, former state senator and lobbyist extraordinaire for 40 years. Through that time, whenever a Statehouse reporter has asked legislators to list the most influential (or simply best) lobbyists, Roden has nearly always come up on top, far above everyone else.

And that round of thumbs up doesn't come by virtue of his clients, who may in general be well-heeled (phone companies and various alcohol and tobacco firms among others have retained him) but aren't always naturally influential sources of power on their own. When it comes to persuading the Idaho legislature to do something, Roden has for decades been considered the top pick by far. That surely translates to placement on this list.

Because his was only one influence among many in any single legislative decision, attaching specific achievements may be dicey. But Roden's have accumulated impact over 40 years.

Roden was born in Camas, Washington, in 1929. He graduated from the University of Idaho with degrees in political science and law. Following law school, he served in the U.S. Army as a special agent in the Counter-intelligence Corps. He began acquiring knowledge of state and local government, first as a deputy prosecuting attorney for Ada County and the as an assistant attorney general for the state, where he covered such diverse areas as the Departments of Finance and Law Enforcement and the Public Utilities Commission. He was elected Ada County prosecuting attorney and served one two-year term before successfully running for the Idaho Senate. He concluded his four Senate terms as Senate majority leader.

Some years after leaving the Senate, Roden began to focus much of his law practice on legislative affairs. He was one of the first Idaho lobbyists to represent multiple clients and paved the way for scores of lobbyists who have followed in that path. During much of his career his highest profile clients have been the "sin industries" of alcohol and tobacco. In a socially conservative state where alcohol and tobacco are not held in high esteem, he successfully kept their tax rates among the lowest in the nation.

Because of his deep knowledge of state law and his institutional memory of state policy making, he has been highly successful in working through extremely complex issues and successfully drafting and obtaining approval for legislation relating to those issues. One of the best examples is with the Idaho Telecommunications Act of 1988. This created a complete overhaul of state law relating to the telecommunications industry and, to a great extent, the de-regulation of that industry.

84 H. Westerman WHILLOCK

February 9, 1904 – August 9, 1992. Broadcasting executive. Mayor. Boise.

Much of what is taken for granted by Boise residents and visitors today came about, in part, because of the efforts of a single individual, Henry Westerman "Wes" Whillock. His fingerprints are on the establishment of the Boise airport, Boise State University, KBOI radio and TV, the Association of Idaho Cities and much more.

Whillock was born in Humansville, Missouri, on February 9, 1904. When he was still a child, his family moved to Medford, Oregon, where he graduated from high school. In 1925 he graduated from Oregon State College, with honors. He worked as a traveling salesman for Munsingwear for several years before settling in Boise in 1931 and opening a shoe store. He also became quickly involved in the community. In 1939 he became president of the Boise Chamber of Commerce and helped to lead the effort to establish Boise Junior College. He also worked with other community leaders to relocate the Boise airport to its current location. That relocation freed-up the original airport site to become the campus for the new junior college, and eventually Boise State University.

In 1941, he was elected mayor of Boise. He pushed through adoption of a restaurant health code ordinance, establishment of a city-county health unit, adoption of a Grade A milk ordinance, and the establishment of Bogus Basin ski area. He also was involved in establishing the Idaho Municipal League (now the Association of Idaho Cities) and served as its first president. That was all in the space of about a year; with the arrival of World War II, he resigned as mayor and went on active duty with the U.S. Navy, serving as military officer for the Idaho Selective Service. At the end of the war he was serving in a military government assignment in Korea.

Back in Boise in 1946, he was selected by the Boise city council to serve out the term of former mayor Sam Griffin, who had resigned. During the next two years, Whillock focused on street and bridge improvements, the design and location of the city's first sewage treatment plant, new building codes, and organizing a city airport commission to accept the transfer of the military air base at Gowen Field and establish it as a division of the city.

After leaving city office, he founded a broadcasting company that owned KBOI radio and TV. With his interest in community affairs, local news became a top priority for his radio and TV stations. For many years they employed news staffs that were the largest in Idaho, outside of the *Idaho Statesman*. He also underwrote the merger of two Idaho weekly newspapers, the *Intermountain* run by Perry Swisher of Pocatello and the *Idaho Observer* run by Sam Day of Boise. The merger created the *Intermountain Observer,* which operated from 1967-73 and was the state's leading "liberal" newspaper.

Whillock finally sold his broadcasting interests and retired.

He was one of Boise's most consequential majors, one of its most important broadcasting executives and an important benefactor of Idaho journalism during one of its most vital periods.

85 A.D. FOOTE/ A.J. WILEY

Foote: Engineer. Boise.
Wiley: Engineer. Boise.

First came the gold finds in the Boise Basin around Idaho City, and then the fort downhill, below the foothills, called Fort Boise (as opposed to, and unrelated to, the earlier trading outpost near Parma). Then a settlement around the fort, with state and federal government activities and commercial interests linking the Oregon Trail routes with the roads headed up into the mountains, toward the mines. Then, in small, discrete areas near the modest streams – especially the Boise River – some farming, with the aim of growing crops to help feed the mining communities up in the mountains.

In terms of the growth of Boise, there things stayed for a while, because beyond those river bank areas lay little but sagebrush-covered desert. Farmers figured out that the soil was amenable to crops, but getting the water there, in quantity ... that was an issue. As was the decline of the Boise Basin mines, starting in the 1870s.

Arthur Foote was a mining engineer in the Wood River Valley when he began to consider what would happen if the Boise River could be made to supply water for irrigation far beyond its banks. He persuaded a group of investors in New York that, with a railroad (the Oregon Short Line) soon to be running near Boise, a large irrigation system serving the desert south and west of the city would be profitable. In 1882 investors formed the Idaho Mining and Irrigation Company to underwrite delivery of water, with the idea of buying land and reselling it to farmers, and otherwise profiting from the development.

Foote was right. The Reclamation Service's Boise Project, which diverts water from the river into the New York Canal and across to Lake Lowell and beyond, proves that. But Foote's own diversion dam and New York Canal, now submerged by the backwaters of the later Diversion Dam, were stymied by reluctant investors. The financial Panic of 1893 turned the project into a nightmare of endless lawsuits, failures to pay, and transfers of ownership.

That the system ultimately did emerge can be attributed in great part, however, to the two men who worked together on the effort: Arthur DeWint Foote, hired by the New York investors as chief engineer, and Andrew J. Wiley, who worked for Foote for many years and eventually took over the Idaho projects from him. Foote was the visionary and innovator; Wiley, who was also considered a national expert on dam construction and safety, was the practical engineer who found ways to make those ideas real.

The New York Canal was the first of their critical joint efforts, but not the last. In 1894, with mining activity in the Owyhee Mountains still running strong, Foote was asked by J.M. Guffey to figure out a way to bring electricity – generated from hydropower – to the mines around Silver City. He and Wiley, working with engineers from Andrew Mellon's Pittsburgh Reduction Company (now Alcoa) settled on Swan Falls, about 28 miles from Silver City, and Wiley soon completed the project. Swan Falls provided power for the mines, and later sent juice to the Nampa and Boise areas. The project was literally groundbreaking – not many people other than Foote and Wiley would, at the time, have had the chops to pull it off.

Swan Falls was one of Idaho's most consequential dams. It was the first dam on the Snake River, and the first hydroelectric dam – it showed the way for construction of many others to come. It wiped out steelhead and salmon runs above it in the Snake River system. And it would be the focus of a lawsuit that led to the Snake River Basin Adjudication, a reordering of water rights throughout almost all of Idaho.

86 Dick EARDLEY

December 23, 1928 – June 30, 2012. Journalist. Mayor. Boise.

Dick Eardley, Boise's only mayor to serve three terms (though the incumbent as this is written, David Bieter, has been elected to a third term), had the bad luck to be long identified with a failure: The great white whale he never harpooned: the downtown Boise regional shopping mall that was supposed to revitalize a seriously troubled urban core. Piling insult on top of that, as soon as that approach was declared dead and buried, and a regional mall was built miles away, downtown Boise seemed to spring alive, as if anew.

Many Boiseans from during and after the Eardley years may shorthand the time as the downtown development wars that Eardley lost, but the description is both incomplete and unfair. Eardley drove the transition of Boise from a relatively quiescent period to one of strong growth. Years before the downtown battles, Eardley already had been a significant transitional leader.

He pointed out that although he doggedly pursued the downtown regional mall concept for most of his tenure, he and the city council had abandoned it well before he left, and had set the pattern for both a different (and successful) type of downtown development, and the new mall in western Boise.

Eardley's largest impact, though, probably was at the other end of his political career.

In the 1950s and 1960s, Boise was growing economically but was stagnant in other ways. Its downtown seemed to be in decline, the city was quiet and attracted little attention, and growth was aimed outward, in a steady sprawl. Efforts to correct some of this started as early as 1949 when the Columbian Club proposed a coliseum or auditorium; the city created an auditorium district a decade later, but three more decades would pass until the city actually got one. Efforts to grab hold of city planning and try to aggressively help downtown became the subject of big fights in the 1960s; a time when city hall was held by solidly conservative, and generally anti-planning, officials often involved in either development or real estate. A Boise Redevelopment Agency was established in 1965, but its first acts included demolition of many of Boise's oldest buildings and nearly all of its old Chinatown. Writer L.J. Davis, a former Boisean, famously wrote in a 1974 article in *Harper's Magazine* that Boise seemed to be on the verge of becoming the first city to eradicate itself.

Eardley was a newsman, a Boise television news anchor, during those years. His decision in 1969 to run for the city council was pivotal; he outpolled the mayor (the old-school Jay Amyx) and four years later became mayor himself, with a sympathetic council. In power, he grabbed hold of the city's conflicting urges and brought more rationality to them, setting some long-term policies aimed at limiting, if not banning, sprawl. At the same time Eardley dramatically reformed many of the basic ways the city had long been doing business. He could almost be considered Boise's counterpart to Idaho governor C.A. Robins.

Probably no Boise mayor was front and center for so many dramatic shifts in the city's direction as Dick Eardley.

87 Boyd A. MARTIN

1911 – January 8, 1998. Political scientist, college dean. Moscow.

In 1945, President Harry Truman's schedule wouldn't allow him to participate in the San Francisco Conference to draft the U.N. Charter. Instead, he called Boyd Martin, a 34-year-old political scientist at the University of Idaho, and asked him to represent the president at the conference.

Martin was, without doubt, the most influential political scientist ever to come out of Idaho.

Boyd Archer Martin was born in Cottonwood in 1911 and grew up in Nezperce. He graduated from the University of Idaho in 1936 and went on to receive both masters and doctoral degrees from Stanford where he formed lasting friendships with some of the most influential people of the day, including former president Herbert Hoover. In 1939, when Hitler invaded Poland, Martin accurately predicted that this would lead to a world war. As a result, he and his wife Grace decided to take their life savings of $800 and invest it so that eventually they could fund an institute that would explore the causes of war and the conditions necessary for achieving lasting peace.

During his tenure at the University of Idaho, Martin wore numerous hats – often simultaneously. He served as chairman of the Department of Political Science and then became dean of the College of Letters and Science, the university's largest college. He founded and chaired the Bureau of Public Affairs Research, now known as the James A. and Louise McClure Center for Public Policy. He played the lead role in founding the Idaho Municipal

League, now known as the Association of Idaho Cities. He also played a major role in the work of the Idaho Constitutional Revision Commission, which spent five years drafting a revised Idaho Constitution. (The revised constitution was approved by two-thirds of the members of the Idaho legislature, but then rejected by voters in the 1970 general election.)

Martin also continued to play a significant international role. He was active in President John F. Kennedy's Alliance for Progress, a program designed to improve economic conditions in Latin America. He also wrote or co-wrote nine books and numerous magazine, newspaper, and journal articles.

When Martin retired in 1973, he turned his efforts to the development of the Martin Institute for Peace Studies and Conflict Resolution. The original $800 investment that he and Grace had made in 1939 had grown to over $1 million and served as the basis for an endowment to support the institute. Another element was the establishment of the Martin School of International Studies at the university.

Over the years, Boyd Martin influenced presidents, senators, congressmen, governors, and local officials. He died on January 8, 1998, but his influence has continued through the ongoing work of the Martin Institute, the Martin School of International Studies, the Association of Idaho Cities and the McClure Center for Public Policy Research.

88 Richard BUTLER

February 23, 1918 – September 8, 2004. Engineer. Buried: Coeur d'Alene.

Richard Butler's inclusion on this list should by itself constitute proof that this isn't a list of Idaho's best and wisest—and also not a list of people who most influenced the opinions of Idahoans. National reputation notwithstanding, Butler never appealed to more than a tiny sliver of Idahoans, a cadre numbered in the hundreds rather than in the thousands, even over a period of two decades.

But the impact of his presence in the Idaho Panhandle is impossible to ignore, and some of it—a part of it that was indirect— may even have been valuable.

Richard Girnt Butler was born in Denver and raised in Los Angeles, where he worked independently and with Lockheed Martin in the aerospace industry. He may have become interested in Christian Identity shortly after the end of World War II, but we know that by the early sixties he was a leader of the Christian Defense League—a group led by Wesley Swift, a Ku Klux Klan organizer who in 1946 had founded his own church based on racial identity. After Swift died in 1971, Butler decided to move to northern Idaho and in 1973 launched his own church, the Church of Jesus Christ-Christian, and the Aryan Nations organization.

He set up at a remote spot near Hayden, buildt a compound and attracted followers, typically various stripes of neo-Nazi. Nazi regalia and materials supportive of Adolf Hitler were in ample evidence there. That much might have passed with little notice since anyone seeking the compound would need directions. But Butler also liked publicity. He set up yearly gatherings of the like-minded, and they paraded in downtown Coeur d'Alene. If he wanted attention, he got it, as did Idaho, which picked up an unfortunate reputation as a place where the neo-Nazis go. The group declared bankruptcy in 2000 and had its property foreclosed on to pay a $6.3 million judgment in a civil lawsuit brought by two people who said they were assaulted by Aryan Nations guards in 1998. Butler continued as a public figure even after he lost his compound, until his death at Hayden in September 2004. But, for a time, he and his compound became nearly as identified with "Idaho" as the potato.

The actual number of Aryan sympathizers was almost certainly small, likely never more than a few hundred at a time. When Butler once ran for mayor of Hayden, the result was an extremely lopsided loss – about 2,100 votes to 50. When a lawsuit finally resulted in the takeover and tearing down of the compound, little visible evidence of additional racist culture remained.

There may be a more subtle impact, however. Butler's location in northern Idaho may have signaled the area as one appealing to some whites who had no interest in racist or Nazi cultures but were interested in moving away from more racially diverse or multicultural areas—a degree of white flight. Certainly as a major population influx entered the Idaho Panhandle in the last generation, it was overwhelmingly non-minority.

There has been another effect of Butler's settlement—a counter effect. Idaho long has had a substantial civil rights community, but Butler's arrival and visibility energized many of its activists, especially after incidents in which Butler supporters struck back. The Kootenai County Task Force on Human Relations became one of the most active and respected anti-hate groups in the country, and leaders such as Father Bill Wassmuth and Tony Stewart made their own effective counter-push in the region's culture. Their direct influence may long outlive Butler's.

89 George SHOUP

June 15, 1836 – December 21, 1904. Rancher. Governor, U.S. Senator. Salmon. Buried: Boise, Pioneer Cemetery.

Even had George Washington not done the other things he did – commanding the rebel armies in the Revolution, chairing the Constitutional Convention – he would be entitled to a leading place among the most influential Americans of all time because of his presidency: The first presidency, the one that set so many precedents for all the others.

You can't quite say as much for George Shoup, who was both the last territorial governor of Idaho and the first governor of the state. He spent about a year and a half in the job, counting both the territorial and state positions.

However, he was the man who oversaw the actual governmental transition, never a simple task.

As a politician, Shoup always seemed to be reaching just a little beyond where he was, and in none of the offices he held did he leave a major lasting mark.

As territorial governor, he picked up where his predecessor, Edward Stevenson, had left off; Shoup's call for the Idaho constitutional convention was the one that brought the group together, but it was in fact just a reissuance of Stevenson's.

And Shoup's brief state governorship did little to change the nature of territorial governance. As the incoming state governor, he could have had a big role in picking his lieutenant governor, an important consideration since that person would soon take over the top job. As it happened, that person (the state's second governor), was Norman B. Willey, a complete nonentity unable to effectively handle the job. (Willey was denied a gubernatorial term of his own.)

Shoup then became a U.S. Senator from Idaho, but left no major mark there either.

Still, all these things at such a critical period in Idaho's history do add up. So does Shoup's life outside politics, which was in many ways more interesting: His military adventures in eastern Idaho in the 1860s, which led to defeats of several Indian tribes and in turn to settlement of several areas; and his almost single-handled development of the city of Salmon, which became his home thereafter.

90 | Phil BATT

March 4, 1927 - . Governor, farmer. Wilder.

During his first weeks as governor, Phil Batt was confronted with a complex issue that could have been resolved in various ways. The direction he chose, pushed, and enacted resulted in a path toward clearing removal of nuclear waste from the Idaho National Laboratory near Idaho Falls and, very possibly contributed to keeping that lab alive and giving it a second life.

This was a capstone to Batt's long and intermittent political career—intermittent not because of political misfortune but because he took a breather, from time to time, between offices; as a legislator he never served more than six years in a row. His influence was considerable whether he was in or out of office, from his first election to the Idaho House in 1964 through his departure from the governorship in 1999.

Batt was born at Wilder, raised on a farm there, and became a farmer himself. He grew several crops, most notably hops and onions. He entered politics to follow up the single House term served by his older bother, who decided the legislature wasn't for him. The younger brother became one of Idaho's most effective legislators for decades, and was in state Senate leadership for 10 of the 14 years he was there; those stints included a term as president pro tem. He ran successfully for lieutenant governor in 1978, unsuccessfully (in a close-fought contest) for governor in 1982.

Batt held no office in 1990 when Republicans had their worst political year since 1958, losing a wide range of offices. He stepped in as party chair and bridged many of the conflicts that split party members, leading them toward better organization. The massive

Republican wins in Idaho starting in 1992 owe something to those efforts. Batt himself was a beneficiary of them, winning the governorship in 1994. Three years in, he decided against seeking a second term.

Apart from his work as a political organizer, which has had some lasting effect, Batt's influence has related mainly to two very distinctive areas.

One was helping farm workers and supporting human rights issues. The passage of farm-worker compensation legislation during his term as governor is something that might not have happened had anyone else been in the governor's office. In an introduction to his memoir, *The Compleat Phil Batt,* journalist Lindy High noted, "...he forced this issue through a reluctant legislature by using every weapon at his command. ... But he was subdued at what should have been a great moment: The signing of the bill into law. He said he had lost some lifelong friends over the issue, and he refused to join with those who were triumphant in victory." Batt's human rights efforts have meshed with some of the reaction to the Aryan Nations' developments in the Panhandle, and helped foster a substantial human rights activist community.

His largest impact as governor, however, was his negotiation and signature of a nuclear-waste agreement with the federal Department of Energy, a subject of hot dispute for years between the state and the feds. The full effect of the agreement, which at this writing still is far from completion, can't be projected accurately. But it did seem to change federal perceptions about the eastern Idaho facility now called the Idaho National Laboratory, which in the early '90s appeared to be spiraling downward and may have been headed toward closure. Since the agreement, INL seems to have regained its footing, has been given new missions, and appears more secure. If the Batt agreement changed that trajectory, it changed much of the future of eastern Idaho.

91 Ernie STENSGAR

Tribal leader. Plummer.

Not every reservation in Idaho has progressed at the same rate in terms of their economy and living conditions. Some still struggle, and some have made substantial progress toward building wealth and a better standard of living. You can see the improvements at the commercial and gaming developments of the Kootenai Tribe at Bonners Ferry, where the tribe is in a close-knit partnership with other local entities, the Shoshone-Bannock Tribes' new developments including a major resort center at Fort Hall and the Nez Perce at Hatwai, Kamiah, and other locations.

But the most rapidly-developing tribal commercial and social structures are those of the Coeur d'Alene Tribe, south of the like-named city and southwest of the like-named lake. No one person accounts wholly for that, but the central driving force during the key years of planning and development was Ernie Stensgar.

Stensgar became chairman of the tribe in May 1986 and held the job until an electoral defeat in 2004. By then, he had presided over a transformation affecting not only the tribe, but also the region, and not only the region's economic development but concerns ranging to health care and beyond.

The reservation was a quiet place entering the eighties. The development of a large (and ultimately successful) casino may have been a fairly obvious step in light of similar developments by other tribes. But Stensgar and other tribal leaders did not stop there. They supported a large range of planned economic development (such as the Circling Raven golf course and a large hotel that has hosted quite a few major events), much of which has materialized, and is transforming a rural and traditionally economically troubled area. The tribe employed a handful of people a generation ago; now it employs more than 1,000, one of the largest employers in northern Idaho.

Equally significant are its Benewah Medical Center, slated for a major expansion, and its wellness center, which treat thousands of people beyond the tribe and have set a distinctive approach to health care—one that could reverberate through the region.

In the context of all that, the tribe's successful lawsuit for ownership of the southern third of Lake Coeur d'Alene, won at the U.S. Supreme Court, takes on a more dramatic light.

Ernie Stensgar was the tribal leader when these things either happened or were set in motion. Some of them may have happened without him, but the scope of ambition suggests that his strong presence was a major factor behind this transformation of the Panhandle.

92 Alonzo LELAND

July 12, 1818 - October 24, 1891. Newspaper publisher. Territorial House of Representatives. Buried: Lewiston, Normal Hill cemetery.

If E.D. Pierce can be credited with the discovery of gold in Idaho, then Alonzo Leland must be credited with letting the rest of the world know about it. And the end result is that the combined efforts of these two men opened up Idaho to the world.

In 1860, Alonzo Leland was the editor of the *Portland Times*. When he got word of Pierce's gold discovery, he became a one-man publicity mill spreading the word on the richness of this gold strike. He was so convincing that he convinced himself: In 1862 he quit his job and headed east, settling in Lewiston.

Leland was born in North Springfield, Vermont, on July 12, 1818. He was an 1843 honors graduate in civil engineering from Brown University. After a brief teaching career, he moved west to Oregon in 1850. In Portland, he had a varied career. In addition to his newspaper work, he served as a judge and postmaster, as well as using his civil engineering skills in the planning of Portland.

Once in Lewiston, he became completely immersed in civic activity. He bought a half interest in *The Golden Age*, Idaho's first newspaper. After it closed, he bought the *Lewiston Journal* and then established the *Lewiston Teller*.

When Idaho Territory was organized in 1863 with Lewiston the designated capital, he was elected to serve in the first session of the House of Representatives. When the majority of the territory's population moved south, Leland played a major role in trying to keep the capital in Lewiston. His only success was in using the courts to delay the move by a few months.

He then turned his efforts to creating a new territory that would include northern Idaho, eastern Washington and western Montana. It was a popular concept in the area for some years, and at moments it came close to fruition. Just as he had used his promotional skills as a Portland journalist to publicize the Idaho mines, he used his full powers of both personal persuasion and editorial writing to lead a surge of regional interest in his territorial proposal. He was an effective crusader. In 1887 both the U.S. Senate and House approved legislation creating the new territory and sent it to President Grover Cleveland to sign. Unfortunately for Leland and his forces, Congress had adjourned by the time the bill reached the president and he declined to sign it, which effectively vetoed it. *(For the inside story on Cleveland's veto, see the entry on Edward Stevenson.)*

Leland was a non-stop promoter of the Lewiston area. In the early 1880s, he traveled to Omaha to meet with officials of the Union Pacific to try to convince them to build a rail line up the Clearwater River from Lewiston. Out of that effort, came the eventual decision of one of the UP's leading civil engineers, C.C. Van Arsdol, to move to Lewiston and become the region's most influential highway and railroad design and construction engineer.

Leland died at Lewiston on October 24, 1891, less than two years after Idaho achieved statehood. He is buried in Lewiston's Normal Hill Cemetery.

93 William J. McCONNELL

September 18, 1839 – March 30, 1925. Merchant, lawman. Governor, U.S. Senator. Buried: Moscow, city cemetery.

William McConnell's timing as governor—he was elected to two-year terms in 1892 and 1894—was just bad enough that the state's Republican tradition in the century and more since his governorship, stems not from him but from Republicans who would hold office and develop the party a few years later. But his timing was good in other respects: Taking action in a series of times and places that individually contributed to Idaho's future in small ways, but added up to large changes for the state overall.

He probably was for example, the most important single pioneer in the Payette River valley area, and led its early development. A Michigan native, he moved to California in the gold-strike era, then north to Oregon and in 1863 to the Payette area, just then developing interest as a breadbasket for the Boise Basin mines. McConnell farmed there for a while, and more important, he devised the system of irrigation that made the area from Payette to Horseshoe Bend a rich orchard and row crop area. Also important, in that time of essentially no government services, he was the area's first de facto leader, even serving as a vigilante (and, soon after, as a deputy U.S. Marshal). After a few years, he departed for Oregon, then came back to Idaho, to Moscow, where he set up a department store and took a leading role in the town just as the University of Idaho was struggling through its early years.

McConnell was a large personality, taking roles of leadership wherever he went. (He also served in the Oregon legislature, though he lived in that state only briefly.) He was active in the Idaho constitutional convention, and was well enough regarded to be appointed one of Idaho's first U.S. senators. That was a short term, for only a matter of months, but in 1892 he ran for governor, and won election.

McConnell fell loosely in the progressive camp and associated with the "free silver" advocates among Idaho Republicans—William Borah was periodically an ally, and not coincidentally his son-in-law as well. McConnell's governorship was highly active with new projects. His background in irrigation led him to push for state assistance for a wide range of irrigation projects, which may have helped set the stage for the Carey Act projects in the Magic Valley that bloomed only a few years later. It was his idea to allow for creation of local irrigation districts, and these became busy vehicles for development across southern Idaho in years to come.

He was among the leading supporters of two major pieces of elections legislation during his term, freeing the way (as a practical matter) for both Mormons and women to vote. The Mormon franchise had been made simpler after the LDS Church's rejection of polygamy. Idaho was only the fourth state to allow women to vote, but it had rejected a series of earlier proposals. Strong acceptance and support from the governor were the key ingredients to pushing it over the top in 1896.

McConnell's efforts along these lines soon ran into economic reality: The depression of the 1890s hit Idaho notably hard, and even McConnell personally; his store and house in Moscow were foreclosed on. His Republican style fell out of favor, and the mood had turned much more angry and radical by the time he left office in 1897. The Republican Party at that point, had in fact shattered into pieces and would be reconstructed by more laissez-faire successors.

McConnell returned to Moscow after 1896, and won federal appointments as an Indian inspector and immigration official. He also wrote an early history of Idaho.

94 Nathan FALK

*July 12, 1848, Egenhausen, Bavaria– July 22, 1903
Department store owner.*

Perhaps no early businessman in Boise garnered as much respect as Nathan Falk. The business model he developed would be followed by many successful Idaho businesses long after he was gone.

Falk immigrated from Bavaria to the United States in 1862 and settled in Boise in 1864. He worked as a bookkeeper for the firm of Hessberg and Company and then left to enter into a partnership with his brother David. The Falk brothers operated a small mercantile business on Main Street in Boise. As the business grew and prospered, they were joined by a third brother, Sigmund.

In 1876, under Nathan's leadership, they built a store in the Payette area that was said to be the only mercantile store between Baker City, Oregon and the Boise Basin. Nearly everyone traveling through on the Oregon Trail in that era stopped at Falk's Store.

Still under Nathan's leadership, the business continued expanding with new stores in outlying communities, including Wilder, Nampa, Caldwell, Twin Falls, and La Grande, Oregon. It was the first mercantile chain to be established and operate in Idaho, and one of the most important commercial ventures in the Northwest. Its simple creed: "Do unto others as you would have others do unto you and do it now."

In addition to being a business leader, Falk was also a community leader. He served on the Boise school board and was a director of the Boise Chamber of Commerce. He was active in

Boise's Jewish community and was one of the original trustees of Temple Beth Israel.

Falk died unexpectedly on July 22, 1903, in Hailey. All Boise businesses closed for his funeral and the Chamber of Commerce, city of Boise, Boise school board, and many fraternal and civic organizations passed resolutions memorializing him. In an editorial, the *Daily Statesman* said: "In the untimely death of Nathan Falk this city and the state of Idaho sustain a loss so great that it seems irreparable. He was one of the foremost business men of the state and occupied a very large place in the commercial and social affairs of the capital city. His interests here were very large, but still larger was the influence that he exerted upon the development of the city and its trade interests, upon its business methods and upon its character as a municipality."

The department store chain that Nathan Falk worked so hard to develop continued into the 1980s. Although the Falks were no longer involved in its management, the chain was eventually known as Falk's Idaho Department Store and finally Falk's ID.

Nathan Falk saw an opportunity to make available to consumers throughout the region quality goods in a wide selection at affordable prices, putting the customer first. It was a model that would be followed in the future by many Idahoans, including C.C. Anderson and Joe Albertson.

95 Len B. JORDAN

May 15, 1899 – June 30, 1983. Rancher, farm implements. Governor, U.S. Senator. Buried: Boise, Cloverdale Memorial Park.

Three of the four governor-senator hyphenates on this list (Frank Gooding, William McConnell, and George Shoup are the others) made most of their impact on Idaho outside the realm of those two offices. Not so Len Jordan, whose effect on Idaho came specifically through his actions in those offices. The actions were many and varied, but the most striking had to do with water.

Elected governor in 1950, Jordan was a relative newcomer to politics and government (previously, he'd been a one-term legislator from Grangeville; he'd been defeated for re-election). His first act was to slash the state budget, drastically; he closed two colleges, in Albion and Lewiston. Many of these actions did not last, but they provided the framework for much of the politics of the fifties and a jumping off pad for the next governor, Robert Smylie. (The Lewiston school was restored and became Lewis Clark State College; the Albion institution never recovered and now sits in ruins.)

The most important thing Jordan did as governor was to provide the push that helped ram through the Idaho Power Company's Hells Canyon dams. It was a big fight in the fifties, with a future far from ordained; Jordan's forceful nature and his background as a farmer living near and above the Hells Canyon area surely had its effect.

In the next decade, Jordan was appointed and then elected (twice) U.S. senator. Gone was the hard-core conservatism of the early '50s; this Idaho Republican battled with Richard Nixon over a number of subjects, and even had doubts about Vietnam. He unquestionably provided cover for Democrat Frank Church, and opposed the effort to recall Church in 1967; Church's re-elections in 1968 and even 1974 were influenced to a degree by Jordan and they worked cooperatively on a number of projects.

But then there was also this dam story:

Near the end of his time in the Senate, Jordan pushed hard for the Teton Dam in eastern Idaho, the last reclamation project he would be associated with. At a time when the Bureau of Reclamation was beginning to scale back its construction efforts, Jordan forced a reversal in this case; and the ultimate (and of course unforeseen) result was the Teton Dam flood of 1976.

Such a wild, varying, and unpredictable record from a politician often considered, and who in hindsight surely was, steady and solid.

96 William C. "Hill" BEACHY

c. 1819 – May 24, 1875. Merchant. Lewiston, Silver City. Buried: Marysville, California.

Of the early settlers who reached Idaho before it became a territory, few are more remembered than Hill Beachy. Less known is the major role he played in the development of Idaho.

Beachy is best remembered for tracking down the gang that murdered his friend, Lloyd Magruder. Magruder was a pack-string operator who ran pack trains between Lewiston and the Montana mines. One night while returning from selling supplies in Montana, four men murdered Magruder and four other men stole his gold and horses. Beachy tracked the men down in San Francisco and brought them back to Lewiston, where they were tried and hanged.

Beachy was born in Lebanon, Ohio, around 1819 or 1820. He left home at age 13 and worked on steamboats on the Ohio and Mississippi rivers, becoming a steamboat pilot. In 1846 he went to Mexico, baking and selling bread to U.S. troops during the U.S.-Mexican war. In 1849, hearing of the California gold discovery at Sutter's Mill, he arrived in San Francisco. He married and he and his wife, Margaret, operated a hotel near Marysville, California.

In April 1861, once he heard about the discovery of gold on the Clearwater River, they moved to Lewiston. There, Beachy established and ran the Luna House, Idaho's first hotel. He also established a stagecoach line running from Lewiston to Walla Walla.

This begins the real story of Hill Beachy and Idaho, not about the Magruder murder case but about his development of much of the state's early transportation system.

In 1864, hearing of mining discoveries in the Boise Basin and the Owyhees, Beachy moved to southwest Idaho. Major battles were underway between California and Oregon interests to determine the best point of supply for these new mines – from Oregon in the west or from California and Nevada in the south. In 1865 Beachy established a stageline running from Unionville, California, to Silver City, Idaho, via Winnemucca, Nevada. That venture was short-lived due to Indian hostilities. He next bought out the Barnes and Yates line running between Boise and Silver City.

He also established a major new mine on War Eagle Mountain in the Owyhees called the Golden Chariot. As his crew tunneled deep into the mountain, they discovered that the owners of the Ida-Elmore mine were coming in from the opposite direction mining the same ore deposit. When the two efforts met, an underground war began. Governor David Ballard called out the militia, in time restoring the peace. Later that year, Beachy sold his interest in the Golden Chariot for $300,000.

But he had not given up on the shipping business. After his mining effort, Beachy established the Railroad Stage Line, connecting Boise and Silver City to the Central Pacific rail line in Virginia City, Nevada. With the establishment of Camp Lyon in Owyhee County—probably at the behest of Beachy and some of his supporters—the military was able to protect this new venture from Indian attacks. It became a great success. Nevada historian Victor Goodwin wrote that "Beachy's Railroad Stage Lines enterprise of the late 1860s and early 1870s, together with his antecedent or auxiliary ventures in this field, was probably the most important single factor in the early growth and development of the territories it served," in southern Idaho and northern Nevada.

Beachy sold his stage interests in 1871 and moved to San Francisco. He suffered a stroke, died on May 24, 1875, and was buried at Marysville. The passing was noted in papers throughout the West; his wife and six of his seven children had died before him.

97 Richard Z. JOHNSON

May 21, 1837 – September 10, 1913 Attorney, Attorney General. Buried in Lindau, Germany.

Richard Z. Johnson was one of Idaho's earliest attorneys and, for most of his career, one of its best known and most successful. He grew up in a political household. His father was the first postmaster of Akron, Ohio, then became the city's mayor and eventually was elected to Congress. Johnson was born in Akron and received his law degree from Yale in 1859. In 1864, he established a law practice in Ruby City, then the county seat of Owyhee County. Idaho Territory was one year old. He soon moved his law practice to Silver City and remained there until 1878, when he moved to Boise.

Johnson was elected to the territorial legislature in 1880 and again in 1882. He sponsored the legislation creating the Boise Independent School District and served for fifteen years on the Boise school board. During this time the district experienced substantial growth and expansion of facilities and programs.

In 1885 he was appointed to the commission that revised and codified Idaho territorial statutes. In 1887 he was appointed territorial attorney general and reappointed in 1889, becoming the last person to hold this position before Idaho became a state in 1890. In 1889, following the establishment of the University of Idaho by the territorial legislature, Johnson was named one of the original members of the university's board of regents. In that position he played a major role in identifying and purchasing land for the campus in Moscow, authorizing the construction of its first buildings and hiring its first president and faculty.

Known to have remarkable powers of concentration and retention, Johnson was one of the territory's finest orators. All of these talents served him well in the practice of law. He was one of the early presidents of the Idaho State Bar and for many years was sought out to serve as counsel in some of Idaho's highest profile cases. An example was his successful representation of the Trade Dollar Consolidated Mining and Milling Company when its Snake River water rights were challenged after the company began construction of Swan Falls Dam. Johnson brought in two other young attorneys as part of his team—William E. Borah and John Nugent, both future U.S. senators.

Johnson owned considerable real estate in Boise, and, in 1885, he constructed a new brick office building with Greek Revival pillars to house his law office. At the time he owned the largest law library in Idaho and most of that library is still on the shelves in the old building, which still stands in the Old Town part of downtown Boise at 112 N. 6th Street.

In 1892 he retired from private practice and began taking annual trips to Germany where his wife was born. Eventually they purchased a house on the German-Swiss border overlooking Lake Constance. He died there on September 10, 1913 and is buried at Lindau, Germany.

Although Johnson left Idaho only two years after statehood was achieved, 130 years later his impact is still felt by members of the Idaho Bar, students, teachers and administrators of Idaho's second largest school district, and students, staff, and faculty at the University of Idaho.

98 Carl E. BROWN

September 10, 1878 – August 20, 1963 Merchant, mining, lumberman. Buried in McCall cemetery.

Carl Brown came from New Hampshire to Idaho in 1903 to look after a mine in which his father had invested. He wound up doing a great deal more, laying the blueprint and imposing many of the specifics within it, for the city of McCall.

Brown was born in Whitefield, New Hampshire, on September 10, 1878. His father owned extensive timber and mill interests in New Hampshire, and Carl came of age with a great love for the timber industry. With his move to Idaho, he would become the dominant figure in the development of McCall.

As a young man in Idaho he tried his hand at mining and farming, but really established himself in the McCall area delivering mail and supplies to remote locations such a Warren and Big Creek. He carried the mail on horseback, by dogsled, on foot, by boat, and eventually by car.

Brown went to work for McCall lumber mill owner Theodore Hoff in 1914 and soon became his partner. For the next fifteen years their operation grew to become the largest employer in McCall. One of their primary customers was the Union Pacific Railroad, which bought ties from them. Then, following the stock market collapse in 1929, orders dwindled and Hoff decided to get out of the business. Brown took over as sole owner and renamed the business the Brown Tie and Lumber Company.

Brown had an interest in politics. He was elected to the Idaho Senate on three occasions and in three different decades: in 1922,

1936 and 1944. He also served as Idaho's Democratic National Committeeman and was a delegate to the Democratic national conventions in 1940 and 1948.

When President Franklin Roosevelt's Civilian Conservation Corps looked to Idaho, Brown was their primary contact for the area. He helped in the siting and construction of camps, recommended routes for roads to be constructed and suggested individuals to hire as supervisors. Today many rural roads in Valley County follow courses originally recommended by Carl Brown to the CCC, which constructed them.

His company survived the depression. Brown built a new and expanded mill following a fire in 1940. He also continued to buy timberland until he owned more than 22,000 acres, although about 80 percent of the timber that ran through the mill was from public lands. In 1949, Brown Tie and Lumber processed 16 million board feet of lumber and processed an additional six million board feet brought from other mills for drying and custom planing. Union Pacific purchased five million feet of railroad ties that year.

The community meant a great deal to Brown. In 1938 he donated 80 acres of land three miles outside of McCall to develop McCall's first public ski area. He also donated lumber for the lodge, ski lift, and ski jump. Ten years later he was president of the board that built and operated Shore Lodge. He donated 40 acres of land to Boise's First Methodist Church to construct a church camp.

But Carl Brown's legacy didn't end with his death. Although the mill is long gone, over the century following his arrival in the McCall area his descendants have continued to have a major impact on the area. Both McCall's hospital and its high school came about with leadership from the Brown family. Brundage Mountain ski area was a collaborative project of the Brown family and J.R. Simplot and is today operated by Carl Brown's granddaughter and her husband.

Carl Brown died on August 29, 1963, and was laid to rest in the McCall cemetery—the appropriate choice since he had after all donated the land on which the cemetery is located.

99 C.C. ANDERSON

November 2, 1873 – December 27, 1958. Department store owner.

There was a time not so long ago when Boise was known as a corporate headquarters town, with Morrison-Knudsen, Boise Cascade, Albertsons, J.R. Simplot Co., and Ore-Idaho Foods, among others located there. Fewer will remember there was also a time when Boise was the headquarters for a major regional department store chain. The chain was C.C. Anderson's.

Columbus Charles Anderson, was born on November 2, 1873, near Osceola, Missouri. In the early 1890s, he worked for the Colorado Golden Rule chain and established his own Golden Rule store in Central City, Colorado. Golden Rule was a loosely knit chain of retail merchants that provided quality, low-priced goods sold on a cash basis. Prices were kept low through volume purchasing by the stores.

In 1896, Anderson moved to Boise and opened a Golden Rule Store on Main Street. He was 23 years old. He then began branching out and established stores in Idaho Falls, Twin Falls, Lewiston and Buhl. Anderson's primary competition was from a rapidly expanding group of Golden Rule stores owned by Wyoming retailer J.C. Penney. Penney and Anderson were associates and had known each other since the 1890s. Although the Golden Rule franchise was loosely put together, it imposed a rule that a franchisee could not establish a new store in a town that already had a Golden Rule Store owned by another franchisee. To get out from under this policy, both men left the Golden Rule franchise and established independent department store chains. Penney's became the J.C. Penney Company and Anderson's became C.C. Anderson Company.

Anderson's success was based on a number of factors. He required cash payments and avoided credit. He bought in quantity and paid promptly. He also gave cash refunds to dissatisfied customers, a then unheard-of practice. He employed skilled buyers who knew both the national markets and the C.C. Anderson customers.

Anderson continued expanding his business until he had stores in Idaho, Colorado, Utah, Oregon, and Washington. In 1937, Anderson sold his 23-store chain to Allied Stores. Eventually they changed the name to the Bon Marche. When Allied was absorbed by Federated Department Stores, the name was once again changed, this time to Macy's.

As his business prospered, Anderson also took an active role in serving his community. He was president of the Children's Home Finding and Aid Society, and the Boise YMCA, and chairman of the committee formed to bring Union Pacific to Boise. He was also on the board of the Idaho First National Bank. During World War I he served as State Fuel Director and during World War II was director of the Idaho Office of Price Administration. He was also an active member of Boise's First Methodist Church and was one of the major financial supporters for the construction of the Cathedral of the Rockies.

Anderson lived out his retirement in Boise where he passed died on December 27, 1958. The Boise store that had been the anchor for the Anderson chain went through the name changes from C.C. Anderson's to the Bon Marche to Macy's. It was downtown Boise's last department store and closed in 2010. A new owner plans to convert the building to apartments.

100 Merle WELLS

December 1, 1918 - November 6, 2000. Historian. Buried, Pioneer Cemetery, Boise.

You can't write about Idaho history without owing a debt to Merle Wells, the Idaho historian who very nearly created the field in the Gem State. You can't go far in reading about Idaho history either, without bumping up against his contributions. Or even go far driving around Idaho learning about its history—it was Wells who led the effort to install many of the historic travel markers around the state, and he personally wrote the text for 325 of them.

One newspaper described him as "author, educator, and keeper of the state's historical flame for nearly 30 years"—and in fact much longer.

Born in Canada to parents who were U.S. citizens, Wells came to Boise in 1930 with his parents and was headed toward a career in law when, while at the still-new Boise Junior College, he started studying Idaho history, and was hooked. The pivotal professor, he has said, was BJC President Eugene Chaffee, who is elsewhere on this list, and who hired Wells to teach history there for some years. He wrote plenty of Idaho history himself, much of it in journal articles published around the region, all of it forming a basis for much of what has been written since.

Wells taught at The College of Idaho, his alma mater, during World War II and then completed a doctorate in history at the University of California, Berkeley. But Idaho was home; and after several years of teaching in Pennsylvania, he returned to Boise in

1956 to work at the Idaho State Historical Society. Then, as one speaker at his funeral recalled, "...truth be told, timing is everything, even in the history profession, and it was Merle's good fortune to be on the job for history when states began creating professional archival and records management programs; when states began marking historic sites along the roadways, and when the seeds planted in the Depression years with the Historic American Buildings Survey blossomed into the National Historic Preservation Act of 1966 and the creation of state/federal partnerships in historic preservation. In each of those areas, Merle stepped in and made Idaho part of the national scene. To borrow from the title of Dean Acheson's memoir, Merle was "present at the creation" and made the most of it.

At the time, another report said: "The Idaho state archives was an unorganized pile of papers stuffed into an obscure closet in the Idaho Statehouse when Wells got his hands on it. Not long after his death (though in considerable part because of his efforts) many of those papers now are ensconced in a new historical research building, near the old state penitentiary. Wells founded the *Idaho Yesterdays* magazine, which for more than a quarter century (in fact nearly fifty years) gave visibility to Idaho historical research. He began indexing Idaho newspapers when he was in his late teens."

The state's new archives building is named after Wells.

What we know about something influences us, a lot, toward it. And a lot of what we know about Idaho, we know courtesy of Merle Wells.

And 50-plus honorable mentions

These people—mostly Idahoans, though a few are not—should not be considered numbers 101 to 150 (or so), and to make the point they're listed here in alphabetical order. All of them have had some effect on Idaho, in some cases substantial but in our view less than those on the main list. In some cases, there were disqualifying factors. But when you think about the effect that individual people have had on Idaho, these certainly should not be too far off from consideration.

STEVE ANTONE – Maybe no single legislator ever affected Idaho tax law as much as Antone, who chaired the pivotal House Revenue and Taxation Committee for a very long time. He is one of the main reasons Idaho's 1% Initiative was revised and didn't have the same long-term effects as California's Proposition 13 and is also the primary reason that Idaho's resort cities have local option sales taxes.

BEAVER DICK – Rich Leigh, known as Beaver Dick, operated ferries at two key locations on the Snake River at Boise and Idaho Falls. The development of settlements at those locations was not coincidental.

FRANK BUHL – As the de facto founder and namesake of Buhl and settlement in the nearby area, around to the Thousand Springs, eastern industrialist Frank Buhl was one of the important players in the development of the Magic Valley. And he did visit the area, once. But he never lived in Idaho.

BEN and LEW CASWELL – The Caswells, who moved from Michigan to Idaho in 1894, were principally responsible for Idaho's last big mining rush, in an area where mining has yet to play out. The brothers first came to Cabin Creek and Rush Creek in Valley County, doing a little farming, hunting, and trapping, and pulling in some cash with low-key placer mining. Then they found an unexpectedly large amount, and showed up in Boise in the summer of 1897 with a large haul of coarse placer gold. Over the next five years a rush developed at the Thunder Mountain area, in the mountains east of McCall. Mining goes on in the area, around Stibnite.

PETE CENARRUSA – Pete Cenarrusa was continuously and productively active in elective office in Idaho for close to a half-century, longer than anyone else. In his case there is no single unilateral effect you can point to, no one sweeping change, easily and unilaterally attributable. And yet this is one of those rare cases where the usual rule on influence—someone who decisively changed the way Idaho is—has to be at least bent a little. He has had incremental impact on the way Idaho is run over the period of a lot of years.

You can point to a few areas where his impact was clearly noticeable. His was key support in the mid-sixties for a state sales tax (It likely wouldn't have cleared the House, where he was speaker, without his support). He was a leading developer of the first state legislative staff (and co-hired Myran Schlecte to run it). On the Idaho Land Board, he was a relentless champion of ranching and agricultural interests, affecting the course of that body and state policies over time. Cenarrusa's main contribution to the state may have been a dog that has never barked in the night-time. The state elections office was under Cenarrusa's jurisdiction for decades, and for many years since under his successor and protégée Ben Ysursa (who was Cenarrusa's deputy for elections for many years), and during all that time not a single substantial complaint (note *substantial*, since crackpot complaints do emerge) has arisen concerning the conduct of state elections. It's a job so tough, they've made it look easy.

In addition to his public duties, he has also been strong supporter of activities related to preservation of the Basque culture.

J.A. CHAMBERLIN – The last of Idaho's major highways was Highway 12 from Kooskia east to the Lolo Pass. That road or something like it had been discussed for decades, and at one point, before World War II intervened, there was talk of a highway running along the Salmon River from Salmon to Riggins. The need for such a road was clear: Between Interstate 90 to the north, running through Coeur d'Alene and Kellogg, and Interstate 84 to the south, running through Boise and Pocatello, was about 400 miles of territory in which little east-west transport was possible at a speed much faster than could be gotten from a pack horse. There was no easy or terribly obvious route through this extremely rugged, mountainous country.

In 1930 the Idaho Transportation Department decided to find a way to fix the problem, and dispatched engineer J.A. Chamberlin to map a route for a Lewiston-Lolo road. That is what he did, with some difficulty. Attempts to plot a route by plane failed (as nearly did the plane, on more than one occasion.) Chamberlin in effect had to personally pioneer much of the route to get a sense of how the road could be built, although, fortunately, he had an assist from earlier survey work done by Wellington Bird, Sewell Truax, William Craig and C.C. Van Arsdol. The road did not come quickly or easily; it was finally completed, as a federal highway, in 1962. But a large chunk of the credit for designing it, and even making it possible, goes to Chamberlin.

RALPH COMSTOCK – For most of Idaho history, chain banking—the ownership of local branches by a central bank—has been an important part of the business landscape, but it started out in Idaho history banned under state law. For about half of Idaho's statehood (so far), the most powerful and influential bank in the state has been a regional one, First Security. The man most central to both of these developments is a businessman named Ralph Comstock.

The story of First Security is fundamentally the story of the Eccles family of Utah, which in time bought several small banks in eastern Idaho and a larger one in Nampa. They intersected with the Comstock family, which had founded a small but thriving pioneer bank at Rexburg. The Comstocks were politically well connected through the Frank Gooding-John Thomas Republican organization and, especially, through newspaperman, attorney, and lobbyist Lloyd Adams of Rexburg (who first became a newspaper editor courtesy of Ross Comstock). The Eccleses hired Ross's son Ralph to manage the Nampa bank, then all of the banks First Security bought in southern Idaho. Comstock brought First Security into the heart of Idaho Republican politics, which after intense lobbying influenced the change in law that resulted in chain banking in Idaho. Banks larger than First Security have come along in the years since. But the structural changes Comstock and First Security put in place in Idaho have endured.

PATRICK CONNOR – Connor was the general who founded Soda Springs with a group of about 160 breakaways from the Utah LDS Church (their leader, Joseph Morris, had told Brigham Young he was on the "wrong path," and soon after found himself literally under fire—and dead). That location became a stop on the Oregon Trail, which Connor's layout of the town also encouraged. (Cort Conley wrote a detailed description of how this happened in his book *Idaho for the Curious*).

"DIAMONDFIELD" JACK DAVIS – A big-talking gunman, though his bark seems to have been a lot more fierce than his bite, Davis was a bit player in the cattle and sheep wars that visited Idaho in the late 1800s, though on a smaller scale than those in Wyoming. Davis' arrest for the shooting of two sheep workers brought the cattle/sheep wars to a head in Idaho, helped establish the cattle primacy and drew lines that lasted in the many years since.

Father **PIERRE-JEAN de SMET** – A Jesuit missionary, he ranged wide across the West, seeking to convert Indian tribes to

Catholicism. In some places he was successful, notably among the Coeur d'Alenes in the Idaho Panhandle. *Idaho for the Curious* notes that when he visited the tribe in 1842—which would make his one of the earliest missionary efforts in the region—"...he received an effusive welcome, and Christianity was to have a major effect on the history of the tribe."

In 1762, Coeur d'Alene Chief Circling Raven had a vision that men wearing black robes and carrying crossed sticks would visit the tribe, bringing with them important powers. In 1842 Father DeSmet first visited the tribe and the tribe believed that visit was the fulfillment of Circling Raven's vision. Since that time, Christianity has had a major impact on the history of the tribe.

PHILO FARNSWORTH – A list of Idahoans who had national, or even international, influence would put Philo Farnsworth toward the top: The evidence is that he, more than anyone else, invented television. Though he was born (and died) in Utah, he grew up on a farm in Rigby, where the crop rows helped spark one of the critical breakthroughs he had in developing the television screen. His critical research and development work, however, took place after he left Idaho.

VARDIS FISHER – One of Idaho's leading novelists, who for many years was based at a remote house outside Hagerman, Vardis Fisher was very prolific and wrote practically all of his highly-regarded fiction, and a lot of non-fiction too, in Idaho. He has been well known for decades in literary circles, and the author Thomas Wolfe was a close friend. He was the author of the first volume of the Federal Writers Project's American Guides series, and the Idaho Guide unexpectedly became the model for the rest of the series. His alliance with Caxton Printers in Caldwell kept Fisher in print and boosted Caxton's prestige. Fisher's long-term effectiveness, though, is harder to pinpoint. His best-known novel was *Mountain Man*, which years after his death was made into the movie *Jeremiah Johnson* starring Robert Redford.

JOE GARRY – Coeur d'Alene tribal chief Joe Garry was a national leader in the early '50s fight on tribal termination, with much of the fight starting from the Coeur d'Alene reservation, some of it with legal cases in which he was a personal plaintiff. Tribal termination was a policy proposing that tribal members would be better off being assimilated into general society. It was a large movement, but Garry was clearly the spearhead for blunting the termination effort and realigning tax and other law that related to reservations for many years to come. Garry was more a national than a local figure, but he had some impact regionally as well. Garry was the first Native American to serve in each house of the State Legislature; his niece Jeanne Givens, is a former state representative and a two-time congressional candidate.

A.E. GIPSON – Gipson was the founder of Caxton Printers at Caldwell, which is still owned and run by his family. Initially the editor and publisher of a monthly newspaper (the *Gem State Rural*), he soon began publishing books as well (including one co-written by one of the authors of this book). Caxton's has also been a major regional book printer, delivering many official book-form documents including editions of the Idaho Code and annual session laws as well as election ballots.

GUSTAVUS GLENN – The namesake of Glenns Ferry is partly responsible for the founding of that city, but he had another impact too at a critical moment. Near Glenns Ferry, the Oregon Trail crossed the Snake River, at the Three Island Crossing ford. It was a difficult fording, one of the most feared points along the trail, and a major obstacle on the way west. In 1863 Glenn set up a ferry, a large enough boat to be stable and carry large loads, at a more easily managed point in the river, one that (important in those days) sliced 20 miles from the route west. The city named for that helpful ferry is a few miles downstream from its old route.

HARRY GULEKE – "Cap" Guleke founded many of the runs on the Salmon River and Middle Fork, and first brought the idea of recreational river running to national attention. And made possible some of the initial, isolated, settlement through that area. His first trip was in 1896, he last about 1939. He was the mentor for the earliest collection of river runners who would follow.

ROBERT HANSBERGER – The Boise business leader was the first person in Idaho to form a major conglomerate, to take an existing large business and branch it out into other areas. In his case, he took Boise Cascade, of which he was chief executive office, and converted it in the late '50s and early '60s into a behemoth.

E.H., ROLAND, and AVERELL HARRIMAN – The Harriman family was long associated with Union Pacific Railroad, but that was only part of their Idaho story. E.H. played a key role in Oregon Short Line, and bought the Railroad Ranch property near Island Park. His son Roland saw it converted into state park lands and strongly advocated a state parks department. His son Averell was the major force behind creation of the Sun Valley ski resort.

PAT HARWOOD – By many accounts, the most politically powerful private organization in Idaho may be the Idaho Association of Commerce & Industry. One of its first leaders, and one of its most effective, was Pat Harwood. He was a point man in the business community for selling the referendum on the sales tax in 1966.

ERNEST HEMINGWAY – Hemingway didn't quite meet our criteria for inclusion on the 100 because his impact on Idaho was slight. He did live in Idaho, though not (in accumulated time) as long as many people probably think. For two decades Hemingway was in and out of Idaho and did some of his major writing in the Ketchum area; he wrote much of *For Whom the Bell Tolls* in Idaho. The Silver Creek preserve probably wouldn't exist but for him, and he certainly wound up adding cachet for the Sun Valley area.

DANIEL HURLBUTT – The Snake River Basin Adjudication, started in 1987 and nearing completion as this book goes to press, will have comprehensively assigned water rights to everyone who has one in the Snake River Basin, which is to say, in 87 percent of the state. That determination of water rights is one of the biggest events in deciding where much of Idaho is headed, and what its economy and society will look like, in the century ahead. Daniel Hurlbutt, then a 5th district judge, was assigned to oversee the case when it was launched. Presiding over it for its first dozen, and most contentious, years, he set the path his successors on the case have followed, toward a remarkably successful conclusion. If a quarter-century seems a long time for a law case to take, consider that most water adjudications in western states, most of them covering areas far smaller than this one, have been underway for far longer, with little prospect of conclusion.

CHIEF JOSEPH – One of the best-known of any persons widely associated with Idaho, Joseph (more properly, Young Joseph in recognition of his father, or still more properly Hin-mah-too-yah-lat-kekt) is a revered figure, but his ties to Idaho are actually looser than many people imagine. He considered his home to be in the Wallowa Valley in what is now Oregon around the city now called Joseph, and spent much of his life trying to get back there. He was leader not of all the Nez Perce but of a band called, reasonably, the Wallowa. They were forced off those lands in 1877, precipitating the flight to Canada known as the Nez Perce War. One of the major battles was fought near the current town of White Bird; its name derives from that of one of the Nez Perce chiefs. Joseph, one of the Nez Perce leaders, was one of the leaders (but not the only one, and not the war chief) in the flight across Idaho; his fame came with the surrender in Montana. Joseph never really was an Idaho resident. After the war, he was held in Kansas and Oklahoma before returning to the Northwest – not to Idaho or Oregon, but to northeast Washington state.

ALBERT KLEINSCHMIDT – Copper was found in the Seven Devils (in Adams County, near Hells Canyon) in the 1860s, but not until Kleinschmidt threw money at it did it start to develop. He ran rails in the Seven Devils and established a series of large copper mines; when the rail line proved unsatisfactory for getting the ore out, he built the Kleinschmidt grade. (A test for hard-core Idahoans: Have you ever driven that nail-biter?) Kleinschmidt finally gave up in the area by the turn of the century, but some mining in the Cuprum (Latin for copper) area goes on to this day.

BLAINE LARSEN – Larsen developed the largest agribusiness in eastern Idaho, based at the wide spot on the road called Hamer; a massive farming operation based around potatoes covering thousands of acres (now in three states) best known for its operations in Jefferson and Clark counties. His company web site notes: "When Blaine Larsen put his money down on 80 dry acres of Idaho desert, folks thought he'd never have a crop worth selling." But the soil turned out to be amenable, and Larsen kept control of storage and processing, saying that "until a Larsen Farms potato is in your hands or your distributor's hands, it's in ours." It is a business large enough that it (and Larsen the person) had a huge impact on a large spread of rural eastern Idaho.

MERIWETHER LEWIS/WILLIAM CLARK – If you could consider them "residents" of Idaho, they'd rank high on this list, since their impact is obvious. But on their travels through Idaho, they paused only as long as necessary – and never very long.

ANDREW MELLON – Mellon, a New York millionaire, came to Idaho in the 1870s trading horses and looking at real estate. He became the principal behind the Trade Dollar Mining Company, which built Swan Falls Dam. Mellon and his brother and brother-in-law were principals behind the Oregon-Idaho Land Company, that went along with the Oregon Short Line and developed town sites – Weiser, Payette, Caldwell, Hailey. (His brother-in-law's name was

Caldwell.) But Mellon did not live in Idaho; he had a house in Silver City he used when traveling to the area, but he was never a resident of the state.

JOHN MULLAN – Here's another one of those early travelers through Idaho who were here only briefly and did exactly *one thing*, made one fateful decision, that puts them on this list. That thing: Pushing through the Mullan Road in the North Idaho panhandle, around 1859-60.

MORLAN (MORLEY) NELSON – Nelson was an educator and a falconer and a national figure in conservation circles. His Idaho impact specifically concerned birds of prey. As early as 1958, he was pressuring the Idaho Legislature to place legal protections for raptors in state law, and worked with electric utilities to make their lines more bird-friendly. When the Snake River Birds of Prey National Conservation Area (south of Boise) was set up in 1980, Nelson was one of the driving forces behind it, and behind the World Center for Birds of Prey at Boise, as well. The conservation area now bears his name, as does a Boise elementary school.

JACK O'CONNOR – One of Idaho's best-known outdoors writers, O'Connor lived in Lewiston but wrote for national and international audiences. He was the long-time firearms editor for *Outdoor Life*. Idaho was one of his topics, and he may have been one of the first people to serious promote Idaho's outdoors activities. An interpretative center can be found at Lewiston.

JOE and WARD PARKINSON – The roots of semiconductor giant Micron Technology go back to the Parkinson brothers, who started the company on a small scale in Boise and built it with a string of investors including billionaire J.R. Simplot.

JOHN PEAVEY – In the mid-'70s Idaho saw a major push for improvements in its public records and open meetings laws. John Peavey, a sheep rancher and state senator, was not the only backer of these measures; he was one of the prime organizers and front men. And he was also one of the lead plaintiffs in the lawsuit that led to the Swan Falls Supreme Court decision in 1982, and the later Snake River Basin Adjudication.

CHIEF POCATELLO – The city's namesake, Chief Pocatello led the Shoshone in their last pre-reservation days, and was one of the negotiators for forming what became the Fort Hall reservation. He was also involved in a mass Mormon baptism in Utah, where his band settled for a brief time.

RON RANKIN – A conservative rooted in Orange County (California) Republican politics, Rankin's first foray in Idaho – a 1967 attempt to recall Senator Frank Church – failed spectacularly. Over the years, however, and focusing more on local and tax issues, Rankin had more effect. He was one of the builders of the strong anti-tax climate in Idaho, and after many unsuccessful runs for office, sometimes as an independent—in which role he once ran for governor—he finally became a Kootenai County commissioner. But his real influence came as a populist agitator, the results of which are still highly visible in the Idaho Panhandle.

VERN RAVENSCROFT – Probably few people singly personified so many of the political and temperamental changes Idaho went through in the mid-20th century as Vern Ravenscroft. A businessman based at Tuttle, near Gooding, he was for some years a conservative Democrat, serving as such in the Idaho legislature. In the late '60s, as the Democratic Party turned more liberal and the Republican more conservative, Ravenscroft began to feel out of place; when he ran for governor in 1970 he lost to Cecil Andrus in the Democratic primary. Two years later, Ravenscroft switched parties, became Republican chairman, and in 1978 ran for governor again, as a Republican—and again failed to win his party's nomination.

He was, after that, probably the central and most visible figure in the state's Sagebrush Rebellion of the early '80s. But his interest in resource issues spread more widely than that; he was also an early advocate for regional aquifer recharge and development of small-scale (low-head) hydropower, and also ran the state's Carey Act organization for many years.

RUBE ROBBINS – Idaho had its definite Wild West period but it seems not to have had quite as many great shoot-'em-up stories as many other western states. Maybe Orlando "Rube" Robbins, the foremost lawman in Idaho during the territorial period, was one reason why. First putting on his deputy sheriff badge in 1864 at Boise, he was still an active lawman—though mainly serving as a guard for prisoners under transport—when he died in 1908.

THEODORE ROOSEVELT – The wildlife refuges, forest presences that ended up as the national forests, all of the early forest management activity—most of the early forest activity in Idaho was generated by the Roosevelt administration. TR, prior to becoming president, spent a fair amount of time in the Panhandle.

LOUISE SHADDUCK – Idaho didn't really get into the business of promoting itself until the late 1950s. That was when Louise Shadduck, who had already by then worked for three Idaho governors and two members of Congress, became the state's first Secretary of Commerce and Development, and was one of the first people to put the state on the map. In later years, she wrote a pile of books about Idaho—about its premier sheepman (Andy Little), medicine in Idaho, rodeos and more. She was also a major organizer behind locating the national and world Boy Scout jamborees at Farragut Park.

RALPH SMEED – In the latter third of the 20th century, and into the new one, Canyon County has emerged as a real political powerhouse in Idaho, regularly producing governors and senators, many sharing a very specific ideology, a collection of ideas, slogans, ways of speaking. The planter of that seed was Caldwell native Ralph Smeed. His father was in the livestock business and owned substantial property in Caldwell, and Ralph took over its management after his father died. After returning from service in World War II, he was introduced (partly by the then-owner of Caxton Printers) to a number of libertarian publications, and Smeed began traveling to national libertarian meetings.

In Caldwell he launched organizations and publications with a libertarian, free-market hard edge. The persistent activity and the development of a much simpler (or simplistic) ideology, with standardized approaches to issues and appearance before voters, had effect. Its first major success was election of Steve Symms to the U.S. House in 1972; by the start of the next decade that approach had become central to Idaho Republican politics. Smeed died in 2010, but his views carry on through many political figures, and the much-seen and sometimes criticized reader board at Caldwell off Interstate 84.

CLINTON DEWITT SMITH – Location of the capital of Idaho in Boise may seem inevitable now, but there was nothing inevitable about it. The first capital of the territory, as visitors to Lewiston are quick to be told, actually was that northern Idaho city. When the capital was assigned there, it was the only sort-of-permanent town in the territory, serving the Clearwater River mining camps. A couple of years later, a similar community (also serving nearby mining camps) named Boise had sprung up to the south. By then, the Clearwater camps had cooled, and Lewiston clung tenuously to its capital status. The territorial legislature passed a bill moving the capital to Boise, but in those early days of loose and easily swayed territorial government, that did not make it a done deal. A lawsuit, in fact, was filed to invalidate most of what that 1864 legislature did.

Into this crisis, in March 1865, stepped newly-appointed Territorial Secretary Clinton DeWitt Smith, the de facto acting governor. Smith turned out to be the first truly decisive leader the new territory had. About a month after his arrival, he gathered the core of the territory's official documents, summoned a military escort from Fort Lapwai, and rode south to Boise. Once there, he declared that the territorial capital had been moved. The move south turned out to be a little less fortuitous for Smith, who died in August 1865 at Rocky Bar, after what one report described as "too strenuous a chess game." His death, in the absence of a territorial governor, effectively left the new territory with no official leadership at all.

HENRY SPALDING – Some historians of Idaho have given a fair amount of attention to Henry Spalding, and you can understand why. Spalding's list of "firsts" was considerable. With his wife Eliza he was one of the first missionaries (he was a Presbyterian minister) to plant themselves in the inland West, with the idea of converting Native Americans to Christianity. Spalding settled in 1836 near Lapwai. He translated part of the Bible into the Nez Perce language, and developed a written version of the tongue (which hadn't existed before). He brought in farming and building equipment previously unseen across a vast region, and also brought in Idaho's first printing press; and he created an irrigation system for the area.

He was also, by many accounts, nearly impossible for most people to get along with. Almost everything he tried to accomplish failed because he kept getting into battles with the natives, other settlers, other missionaries—really, anyone at hand. The American Board of Commissioners for Foreign Missions tried recalling him and then rescinded the recall; Spalding paid no mind. In 1847 the Spaldings moved to the Willamette Valley of Oregon, where they fared better. Their story was dramatic, but their long-term influence on Idaho was not great. Years afterward, after the death of his wife, he came back to the Nez Perce, and retired as a mellower and calmer person. He and Eliza are buried in the Spalding cemetery.

CLIVE STRONG – Attorney Clive Strong is still active and has huge impact in his job running the resources division of the attorney general's office, as this is written – a timing element that keeps him off the main list. But few people in Idaho history have had such effect on Idaho's resources, including water and endowment lands.

BLAINE STUBBLEFIELD – Idaho's communities have many annual events. On a per capita plus notoriety basis, the foremost may be the National Old Time Fiddler's Contest and Festival at Weiser. Weiser had been the home of fiddle events, generally irregular, since 1914, but Stubblefield was the man who institutionalized it, in 1963. It's now a big regional event entering its second half-century.

MATT TAYLOR – In a thin, loose sense Matt Taylor could be considered the founder of Idaho Falls. He built the short bridge across the Snake River at what became Idaho Falls, in 1865. A year later, the area became known as Eagle Rock, and was for some years a regional rail stop until Pocatello took it away. Idaho Falls had no single, definitive founder,

JACK TINGEY – Any number of people move to a new place with an idea for a profitable new business there. Jack Tingey, with his wife Selma, was one of Idaho's most successful. In Utah he had been a fish and game commissioner, and came across the idea of raising fish—mass producing them. No place in Utah seemed suitable, but in 1928 he came to the Thousand Springs area near Buhl to take advantage of the mass of fresh spring water there. He founded the Snake River Trout Farm, out of which grew one of the Magic Valley's premier industries: Trout farming.

DANIEL TUTTLE – Episcopal bishop of the district of Idaho from 1866 to 1886. Tuttle was of the leaders in forming the church establishment in Idaho's early territorial days. It may not be coincidental that the Episcopal church he founded was the creator of what eventually became Boise State University. He was the chief planter of Episcopal churches throughout the region (he was in his 30s at the time).

JOHN VOLLMER – This statehood-era millionaire and banker seemed to have all the goods for leaving a major namesake or two in Idaho: Enough money to buy (at bankruptcy sale) 32,000 acres of Idaho land, and enough clout to guide the development of the Northern Pacific Railroad. He tried using that pull to found a settlement east of Moscow; when homesteaders moved in, they rejected the name "Vollmer" and chose "Troy" instead. In 1905 he directed rail lines in Lewis County away from the struggling new town of Ilo, and platted a new settlement called Vollmer. Long-running conflict (for more than a decade) between Ilo and Vollmer ensued; finally, the two were merged, and took the name Craigmont (after the William Craig in the 100 list). Put Vollmer down on the list of those who couldn't buy a namesake.

TROY WADE – On one level, Troy Wade was another federal bureaucrat sent in from Washington to try to corral the herd of cats then known as the Idaho National Engineering Laboratory. Nowadays, a couple of decades after his tenure there, the name isn't well known in Idaho. But there's a fair chance that, a half-century from now, Eastern Idaho school children will be taught that Wade was the man who saved the research program at Idaho Falls and transformed the Eastern Idaho economy. Or maybe not. But the suggestions of his impact already are considerable. He was the man who switched course for the INEL in a significant way. Before he came, INEL was sealed-off, interacting little with the rest of Eastern Idaho. Wade pushed through a new policy of technology transfer, the sharing of and spinning off of research knowledge and activities to local private businesses before this became general policy at the Department of Energy. That policy has already had considerable effect in Idaho Falls and Pocatello. It has involved local residents much more deeply with the installation. It has helped broaden the INEL mission.

FREDERICK WEYERHAUSER – He was the power behind figures like William Deary and the Humbirds. He had some family members in Idaho who were major players in the Potlatch Corporation, and he owned a massive swath of the state. A lot of northern Idaho developed along lines he set up.

NATHANIEL WYETH – Builder, owner, and manager of the Fort Hall that is on the Fort Hall Reservation, west of the town of Fort Hall (confusing?). He built it in 1834 and lasted two years, until the Hudson's Bay Company bought him out. But by then it was a major and established stop for the Oregon Trail people; much less pivotal for what came after than Fort Boise (*see Francois Payette*) to the west, but still important. And it lasted until 1855.

MAX YOST – For decades, if Yost didn't sign off on a tax measure, it went nowhere. He was one of the best lobbyists in Idaho history, and founder of the Associated Taxpayers of Idaho in 1946. For the better part of four decades he was the central figure in development of tax policy. And during much of that time he presented himself as simply a supplier of tax information, as opposed to a lobbyist. But legislators tended to understand the subtleties involved.

Timeline

1805 – Meriwether Lewis and William Clark vist Idaho on their explorations west, passing through the state from August to October.

1809 – David Thompson of Canada sets up Kullyspell House near Sandpoint, as a trading center.

1829 – Major fur trading rendezvous held in the Teton Valley.

1834 – Fort Boise established by Hudson's Bay Company near Parma.

1836 – Henry Spalding founds an Indian mission at Lapwai, establishes first Idaho school, prints first Idaho book, constructs Idaho first irrigation system and grows first Idaho potatoes.

1843 – Travel along the Oregon Trail, the first major throughway in Idaho, begins in earnest.

1846 – Northwest boundary dispute with Great Britain resolved.

1855 – Mormons from Utah briefly establish a settlement in the Lemhi Valley; it lasts about three years.

1860 – Franklin, the oldest town in Idaho, is founded by Mormon settlers just north of the Utah line.

1860 – A gold find by E.D. Pierce leads to a gold rush near Orofino.

1861 – Lewiston was established, as a commercial center for the Clearwater mining district.

1862 – George Grimes, Moses Splawn and others find and launch mining efforts in the Boise Basin near Idaho City.

1863 - A prospecting party led by Michael Jordan discovers gold at Discovery Bar in the Owyhee Mountains near Silver City. Owyhee County become Idaho's first established county.

1863 – Ft. Boise is established by the Army, leading to the establishment of the city of Boise as a service community for the Boise Basin mines.

1863 – Idaho Territory was created. The first general election is held.

1864 – Boise was formally named capitol of the territory.

1864 – The Idaho Tr-Weekly Statesmen begins publication.

1869 – Fort Hall Indian Reservation was declared.

1974 – Idaho's first daily newspaper, the Owyhee Daily Avalanche, and Idaho's first telegraph system established in Silver City.

1877 – The Nez Perce War began, and ended.

1880 – A rush for lead and silver hit the Wood River Valley.

1882 – New York Canal near Boise begins construction.

1883 – Rexbrg is founded by a Mormon contingent led by Thomas Ricks.

1884 – Major metals discoveries launch development of the Coeur d'Alene mining district (the Silver Valley).

1887 – The first electric light plant starts operation at Hailey.

1889 – A constitutional convention is held at Boise and devises a prospective state constitution. It is approved by popular vote.

1889 – Territorial legislature approves establishment of the University of Idaho at Moscow.

1890 – Idaho is admitted as the 43rd state.

1892 – Violence erupts and martial law is imposed in many of the Silver Valley mines.

1895 – The first comprehensive irrigation law is passed.

1903 – The first Carey Act land openings in Idaho were made.

1905 – Former Governor Frank Steunenberg assassinated.

1908 – Abut half of Idaho was designated as national forest land.

1913 – The Public Utilities Commission and first comprehensive tax and motor vehicle laws were passed.

1916 – Idaho adopts liquor prohibition by constitutional amendment.

1922 – Idaho first radio station, KFAU, established at Boise High School.

1936 – Sun Valley was developed as a ski resort.

1938 – Highway 95, the Idaho north-south highway, was paved in full.

1943 – Mountain Home Air Force Base opened.

1947 – Public schools were reorganized, and Idaho State University established at Pocatello, under legislative action.

1949 – The National Reactor Testing Station (NRTS), with headquarters at Idaho Falls, was established.

1951 – World's first use of nuclear power to generate electricity at NRTS.

1953 – The first television broadcast in Idaho started at KIDO-TV (later KTVB-TV) in Boise.

1955 – Idaho Power Company obtains a license to build three dams in the Hells Canyon area.

1962 – The last major Idaho highway, Highway 12 from Lewiston east to Missoula, is completed.

1963 – The Legislative Council (staff) is created.

1965 – A state sales tax is adopted, and a parks department and water resource board created.

1969 – Beginning of annual legislative sessions.

1970 – Idaho voters reject revised Idaho constitution.

1974 – Boise State College becomes Boise State University.

1976 – The Teton Dam collapses, and large areas in eastern Idaho, including Rexburg and Idaho falls, are flooded.

1978 – Voters pass the 1% property tax initiative.

1980 – The River of No Return Wilderness (the name of Frank Church was added later) adopted by congressional action.

1987 – The Snake River Basin Adjudication gets underway.

1990 – Idaho celebrates 100 years of statehood.

Bibliography

To begin, a hat tip to the *Idaho Yesterdays* magazine, which over the years has added a lot to our understanding of Idaho. Two specific articles should be noted here; "A Mormon transition in Idaho politics," by Leo Lyman, from Winter 1977 (especially useful on the profile of William Budge), and "A Kingmaker's King," by Bud Davis, Summer 1968 (the only extensive single profile of Lloyd Adams), but many have been valuable over the years.

The basic reference on Idaho government, and much more, is the Idaho Blue Book, published biennially by the Idaho Secretary of State's office. It should be on every Idahoan's book shelf.

Ridenbaugh Press has published a series of books on Idaho government and politics. *Paradox Politics* (1988) was a history of Idaho politics focusing on the half-century before its publication; a second edition with updating notes was published in 2009. For detailed political review, the *Idaho Political Almanac*s of 1990, 1992, 1994 and 1996, and the *Idaho Yearbook/Directory* volumes for 1998, 199, 2000 and 2001 are recommended.

A string of useful memoirs and biographies on Idaho political figures – including Robert Smylie, Cecil Andrus, James McClure, Frank Church, Phil Batt, Pete Cenarrusa, Byron Johnson, Don Samuelson, and others, have emerged in recent years, and these are all well worth review.

Here are some o the books on Idaho we found useful in preparing this book – and in learning about Idaho generally.

– , *The Blue Book of Owyhee County (1898)* Owyhee County Historical Society reprint

– , *Idaho Almanac*, Idaho Department of Commerce and Development, Symms York Co. (1963)

–, *Idaho Blue Book,* Secretary of State (various editions)

–, *Idaho's Highway History 1863-1975*, Idaho Transportation Department (1975).

–, *Illustrated History of Idaho*, The Lewis Publishing Company (1899).

Cecil Andrus and Joel Connelly, *Politics Western Style*, Sasquatch Books (1998).

Rick Ardinger and Martin Peterson, *Celebrating Idaho,* The Caxton Printers Ltd. (1991)

LeRoy Ashby, *The Spearless Leader: Senator Borah and the Progressive Movement in the 1920s*, University of Illinois Press (1972).

LeRoy Ashby and Rod Gramer, *Fighting the Odds: The Life of Senator Frank Church*, WSU Press (1994).

Phil Batt, *The Compleat Phil Batt, a Kaleidoscope* (no publisher noted) (1999).

Carl Bianchi (editor), *Justice for the Times*, Idaho Law Foundation (1990).

Karl Boyd Brooks, *Public Power, Private Dams: The Hells Canyon High Dam Controversy*, University of Washington Press (2006).

Warren Brown and Jane Brown, *It's Fun to Remember: A King's Pines Autobiography,* Warren Huffington Brown (1999)

John Corlett (editor), *Idaho Almanac,* Idaho Division of Tourism and Economic Development (1977)

Chris Carlson, *Cecil Andrus: Idaho's Greatest Governor*, Caxton Press (2011).

Eugene B. Chaffee, *Boise College: An Idea Grows*, Syms-York Company (1970).

Linda Campbell Clark, *Nampa, Idaho 1885-1985,* Pacific Press Publishers (1985)

David Cannadine, *Mellon: An American Life,* Alfred A. Knopf (2006)

Zona Chedsey and Carolyn Frei (editors)*Idaho County Voices,* Idaho County Centennial Committee (1990)

Dennis Colson, *Idaho's Constitition: The Tie That Binds*, University of Idaho Press (1991).

Cort Conley, *Idaho for the Curious*, Backeddy Books (1982).

Samuel H. Day, *Crossing the Line – From Editor to Activist to Inmate*, FortKamp Publishing Company (1991).

Dick d'Easum, *Dowager of Discimpline, the Life of Dean of Women Permeal French,*The University Press of Idaho (1981)

Fred T. Dubois, (Louise Clements editor),*The Making of a State,* Eastern Idaho Publishing Company (1971)

John Fahey, *The Days of the Hercules,* The University Press of Idaho (1978)

John Gerassi, *The Boys of Boise: Furor, Vice and Folly in an American City*, University of Washington Press (1st edition 1965).

David H. Grover, *Debaters and Dynamiters: The Story of the Haywood Trial*, Caxton Printers (1964).

John Hailey, *History of Idaho,* Symms York Company (1910)

James A. Hawley, *History of Idaho: The Gem of the Mountains* (3 volumes), S.J. Clarke Publishing Company (1920)

William D. Haywood, *The Autobiography of Big Bill Haywood,* International Publishers (1929)

Byron Johnson, *Poetic Justice: A Memoir*, Limberlost Press (2012).

Grace E. Jordan, *King's Pines of Idaho,* Kirkwood Publishing (first paperback edition 1998)

Grace E. Jordan, *The Unintentional Senator*, Syms-York (1972).

Ronald Limbaugh, *Rocky Mountain Carpetbaggers*, University of Idaho Press (1982).

J. Anthony Lukas, *Big Trouble*, Simon and Schuster, 1997.

Michael Malone, *C. Ben Ross and the New Deal in Idaho*, University of Washington Press (1970).

Boyd Martin, *Idaho Voting Trends 1890-1974*, University of Idaho (1974).

Marian McKenna, *Borah*, University of Michigan Press (1961).

Betty Penson-Ward, *Idaho Women in History,* Legendary Publishing Co. (1991)

Don W. Samuelson, *His Hand on My Shoulder*, ParBest and Dickoens (1993).

Carl Sandburg, *Abraham Lincoln: The Prairie Years and the War Years,* Harcourt Brace and World Inc. (1954)

Carlos A. Schwantes, *In Mountain Shadows: A History of Idaho*, University of Nebraska Press (1991).

Carlos A. Schwantes, *The Pacific Northwest: An Interpretive History*, University of Nebraska Press (1989).

Louise Shadduck, *Andy Little, Idaho Sheep King*, Caxton Printers (1990).

Robert C. Sims and Hope A. Benedict, *Idaho's Governors: Historical Essays on Their Administrations*, Boise State University (1992).

William L. Smallwood, *McClure of Idaho*, Caxton Press, (2007).

Robert E. Smylie, *Governor Smylie Remembers*, University of Idaho Press (1998).

Susan Stacy (editor), *Conversations*, Idaho Public Broadcasting (1990).

Susan Stacy, *Proving the Principle: A History of the Idaho National Engineering and Environmental Laboratory: 1949-1999*.U.S. Department of Energy (200)

Randy Stapilus, *It Happened in Idaho*, Globe-Pequot Press (2001, 2010).

Randy Stapilus, *Outlaw Tales of Idaho*, Globe Pequot Press (2008).

Randy Stapilus, *Paradox Politics: People and Power in Idaho*, Ridenbaugh Press (1988, 2009).

Perry Swisher, *The Day Before Idaho*, News Review Publishing, 1995.

Glen Taylor, *The Way It Was With Me*, Lyle Stuart (1979).

Ted Van Arsdol, *Railway Pathfinder: The Story of C.C. Van Arsdol, 1851-1941,* T. Van Arsdol (1971)

James Weatherby and Randy Stapilus, *Governing Idaho: Politics, People and Power*, Caxton Press (2005).

Tim Woodward, *Tiger on the Road: The Life of Vardis Fisher*, The Caxton Printers (1989).

George Yost and Dick d'Easum, *Idaho the Fruitful Land,* Sims York (1980)

George C. Young and Frederic J. Cochrane, *Hydro Era: The Story of Idaho Power Company*, Idaho Power Company (1978).

Index

Adams, Lloyd 6
Ailshie, James 21
Albertson, Joe 52
Alexander, Moses 77
Anderson, C.C. 231
Andrus, Cecil 43
Antone, Steve 235

Ballard, David 155
Barnes, Verda 159
Barnett, Gwen 87
Batt, Phil 213
Beachey, Hill 225
Beaver Dick 235
Benson, Ezra Taft 68
Boone, William Judson 128
Boise, Tom 99
Borah, William 169
Bowler, Bruce 162
Brown, Carl 229
Budge, Alfred 178
Budge, William 36
Buhl, Frank 235
Butler, Richard 209

Campbell, Bill 153
Cartee, Lafayette 64
Caswell, Ben 236
Caswell, Lew 236
Cenarrusa, Pete 236
Chaffee, Eugene 93
Chamberlin, J.A. 237
Chance, Don 113
Chief Joseph 242
Chief Pocatello 245

Church, Frank 38
Clagett, William 17
Clark, William 243
Cobb, Calvin 118
Comstock, Ralph 237
Connor, Patrick 238
Craig, William 89

Davidson, Georgia 144
Davis, "Diamondfield" Jack 238
Day, Ernie 162
Day, Harry 73
Deary, William 34
DeSmet, Pierre 238
Dewey, William 97
Driscoll, Lynn 140
Dubois, Fred 27

Eardley, Dick 205
Evans, John 184

Falk, Nathan 221
Farnsworth, Philo 239
Fenn, Frank 41
Fisher, Vardis 239
Foote, A.D. 203
French, Permeal 133

Garry, Joe 240
Gipson, A.E. 240
Glenn, Gustavus 240
Gooding, Frank 56
Graue, Erwin 151
Grimes, George 70
Guffey, J.M. 91
Guleke, Harry 241

Hagadone, Duane 75
Haines, John 136
Hailey, John 157
Hansberger, Robert 241
Harriman, Averell 241

Harriman, E.H. 241
Harriman, Rolland 241

Harwood, Pat 241
Hawley, James 95
Haywood, William, D. 130
Hemingway, Ernest 241
Humbird, Thomas 191
Hummell, Charles 173
Hurlbutt, Daniel 242

Johnson, Frank 106
Johnson, Richard Z. 227
Johnston, Bill 54
Jordan, Len 223
Jordan, Michael 147

Kleinschmidt, Albert 243

Larsen, Blaine 243
Lawyer 81
Leland, Alonzo 217
Lewis, Meriwether 243
Little, Andrew 182
Lugenbeel, Pinckney 83

Magnuson, Harry 142
Marshall, Joe 19
Martin, Boyd 207
McClure, James 60
McConnell, William J. 219
McDevitt, Charles 186
Mellon, Andrew 243
Moore, C.W. 62
Morrison, Harry 102
Mullan, John 244

Neil, John B. 197
Nelson, Morley 244

O'Connor, Jack 244

Parkinson, Joe 244
Parkinson, Ward 244
Parker, Aaron 189
Payette, Francois 79
Perrine, Ira 15
Peavey, John 245
Pierce, Elias Davidson 12

Rankin, Ron 245
Ravenscroft, Vern 245
Reberger, Phil 180
Rich, Charles 85
Ricks, Thomas 25
Roach, Tom 23
Robbins, Rube 246
Robins, C.A. 66
Roden, Bill 199
Roosevelt, Theodore 246
Ross, C. Ben 111

Schlechte, Myran 167
Shadduck, Louise 246
Shoup, George 211
Simplot, John R. 32
Smeed, Ralph 247
Smelek, Ray 58
Smith, Clinton Dewitt 247
Smylie, Robert 49
Spalding, Henry 248
Splawn, Moses 70
Standrod, Drew 104
Stensgar, Ernie 215
Steunenberg, Frank 116
Stevenson, Edward 46
Strike, Clifford 149
Strong, Clive 249
Stubblefield, Blaine 249
Sweet, Willis 138
Swisher, Perry 175

Taylor, James "Doc" 164
Taylor, Matt 249

Thompson, David 108
Tingey, Jack 249
Tourtelotte, John 173
Tuttle, Daniel 249
Twilegar, Ron 195

Van Arsdol, C.C. 171
Vollmer, John 250

Wade, Troy 250
Wells, Merle 233
Wetxuwiis 3
Weyerhauser, Frederick 251
Whillock, Westerman 201
Wiley, A.J. 203
Williams, Cal 113
Wyeth, Nathaniel 251

Yost, George 193
Yost, Max 251

The authors

RANDY STAPILUS is editor and publisher of Ridenbaugh Press, edits the *Idaho Weekly Briefing* and the *Snake River Basin Adjudication Digest* and has written a number of books about Idaho, including *Paradox Politics* and the *Idaho Political Field Guide*. He worked for newspapers in Boise, Pocatello, Nampa, Lewiston and Coeur d'Alene, and his weekly column on Idaho politics runs in several Idaho newspapers. After living in Idaho for about 30 years, he and his wife Linda now live in Carlton, Oregon.

MARTIN L. PETERSON served on the staff of Senator Frank Church and was state budget director under Idaho Governors Cecil Andrus and John Evans and a member of the gubernatorial transition team for Governor Butch Otter. He is also a former executive director of the Association of Idaho Cities and served as special assistant for governmental relations for seven presidents of the University of Idaho. Peterson directed the planning and administration of Idaho's state centennial celebration in 1990 and now serves as president of the Idaho State Historical Society's Foundation for Idaho History. He is currently the director of the James A. and Louise McClure Center for Public Policy Research at the University of Idaho.

from
RIDENBAUGH PRESS
www.ridenbaughpress.com

A FREE OFFER

Mention your purchase of this book, and we'll send you the next three editions of the Idaho Weekly Briefing for free.

Just send an email to stapilus@ridenbaugh.com

Order more copies of this book

of **the Idaho 100** directly from the publisher.

You can order from us on our main page at www.ridenbaugh.com

Or, by e-mail at stapilus@ridenbaugh.com

Reach us by phone at (503) 852-0010; or by paper mail at Ridenbaugh Press, P.O. 852, Carlton OR 97111.

IDAHO WEEKLY BRIEFING Our weekly e-mailed report, every Monday morning, on Idaho and how it is changing. Since 1990.

Name _____

Address _____

City _____ State _____ Zip _____

Email _____

Made in the USA
Lexington, KY
01 November 2012